The
Science
of
Intuition

How to
Access the
Inner-net
of Intuitive
Knowledge

NORA TRUSCELLO

ISBN - 10: 1-5441608-7-9
ISBN - 13: 978-1-5441608-7-0

Dedication

To all who intuitively know things,
and don't know how they know, I dedicate this book.

Acknowledgment

This work would not be possible if my father did not profoundly touch my life when I was around fourteen years of age. I was experiencing numerous unexplained occurrences of knowing things, and not understand how I knew. Convinced I was crazy, I turned to my dad for advice. He held out his hand and twisted his wrist, as if turning the knob of a radio. As he did this he gently said, "We are all radios. Some are better conductors than others; you just need to tune into your station." Thanks to my father's advice, I mastered tuning into my intuition.

Table of Contents

Introduction

Have you ever had someone say to you, "I was just thinking that"? Have you been accused of reading someone's mind? Do you feel more tuned in to some people than others? Have you even ignored a premonition to your own peril? We often have kicked ourselves and said, "I knew I should [or should not] have done that!" We all have at least a handful of times in our lives when we felt an urge to do something out of the ordinary but stopped short, only to find out later that it would have been an excellent decision.

Call it intuition or our hunch. It's often thought of as an intangible glimmer, just a random occurrence beyond our control. This is true only because we've never learned to harness the power of intuition.

This book will take you through several exercises designed to make intuition a common occurrence. When you finish reading and applying the exercises, you'll be able to retrieve answers about relationships, finances, health, or anything else you can think to ask. The answers are ripe for picking if you follow the instructions on how to plant the seeds, nurture them, and then harvest the fruits of this gift called intuition.

You may be wondering where these intuitive hunches come from? Why are they almost always right? Most importantly, how can you tap into your intuition? All of these important questions will be addressed in future chapters. A hunch comes out of the blue. We did not manifest it, but we are happy when it arrives. Wouldn't it be great to have a hunch every time we needed it? Should I purchase the house closer to work or the one closer to my family? Is this a good time to ask for that raise? What toy could I get for my grandson's birthday that he will remember for years?

The amount of information we have flowing towards us at any given time is immeasurable. The problem is we don't know how to access all this storehouse of blessings of wealth, love, security, peace, and knowledge. Each of us feels intuitive information, represented by an energetic signature, which I call our Intuitive Footprint™. This Intuitive Footprint™ is unique to each of us and, essentially is our own personal language of intuition.

The Science of Intuition: How to Access the Inner-Net of Intuitive Knowledge will guide you through several techniques that open your intuition, giving you access to this vast storehouse of knowledge.

Scientists are daily discovering evidence that we are not independent observers of a mechanical universe. Rather, because of the intent of our beliefs, we create our own reality. Some of the greatest minds openly admit to using intuition to assist them in their greatest scientific discoveries.

Viktor Schauberger, a pioneer in the study of nature's subtle energies, refused to go to college, believing he would lose his intuitive gifts. Michael Faraday, an English scientist in the field of electromagnetism and electrochemistry, was famous for never giving up on ideas that came from his intuition. Albert Einstein stated "All great achievements of science must start from intuitive knowledge. I believe in intuition and inspiration.... At times I feel certain I am right while not knowing the reason."

Then there was Nikola Tesla known for his contributions to the design of alternating current (AC) electricity supply system. "My brain is only a receiver, in the Universe there's a core from which "We" obtain knowledge, strength and inspiration. I've not penetrated into the secrets of this core, but

I know it exists." Tesla had an advantage over the other scientists; he had been training for decades to maintain his spiritual and creative activity by his highly intuitive mother.

These great scientists connected intimately with a world beyond the visible, using their intuition, to help them formulate new discoveries. With the proper training and understanding, anyone can call upon their intuition and receive accurate clear information. The process is simple. There's a way to know what's in your best interest, what will bring the greatest joy and happiness, even what's the best business deal to close. The answers can come as hunches or as intuition on demand through simple practices.

Why is this possible? How does it happen? Is it accidental? What proof is there it can be so?

Princeton University researcher, Dr. Roger Nelson and colleagues have begun to identify the existence of global consciousness, a mental connectedness we have with each other. Their research is called the Global Consciousness Project. A simple description of this project is as follows. Project researchers attach random number generators to their computers' serial or USB ports. These generate random numbers every second 24 hours a day year after year, and they are being recorded. These computers are all stationed around the world and have no other purpose.

The researchers began to notice that there was a significant statistical deviation from randomness when major events occurred in the world, events like the death of Princess Diana, and the attacks on 9/11.

The following chart, reprinted with Dr. Nelson's permission, plots the random generated numbers from the computers four hours before the attacks on 9/11. Along the x axis are the hours of that day. The small boxes on the X axis represent the times the planes crashed into the buildings. The Y axis represents the variance of the number generators. The higher on the Y-axis, the more variance; the lower on the Y-axis, the less variance. To assist in understanding the significant shift in global consciousness, measured by greater variance in the computer-generated number, pseudo data, based on numbers generated on days without events, was added to the graph.

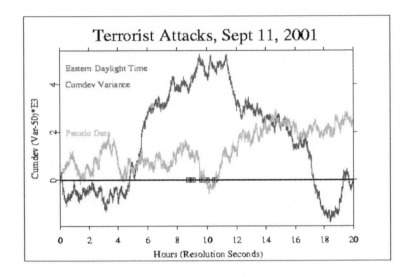

The key is that a few hours before the first attack, these computers started having a greater variance, significantly higher than chance. It was during this time, many people avoided being killed by one of the four doomed flights, or in the World Trade Center. They honored an inner voice, their intuition. Is this proof that global consciousness exists? If you could connect to it, would you be aware of events before they happen? These random number generators may have demonstrated the reality and power of intuition by generating an intensity on September 11, 2001.

Our intuition speaks to us in signs, symbols, feelings, and hunches. Intuition is an excellent source of information coming from an inner knowing. But how is that possible; how can we just know? Arthur Conan Doyle's famous character, Sherlock Holmes, puts it best, "It was easier to know it than to explain why I know it. If you were asked to prove that two and two made four, you might find some difficulty, and yet you're quite sure of the fact." So let's apply some basic elementary questions to these invasive hunches. Who, what, where, when and how do they manifest themselves in each of us and why is it that each of us receives it differently?

We must now ask, "Who has no difficulty in trusting and applying their intuition?" We named a few scientists who trusted their intuition. We've all heard stories of those who did not go to work on 9/11, saving their lives. Nobody questions the existence of many recorded examples of a policeman's instinct when they've stated I've a hunch. Best of all, most women will resoundingly say, "Of course there's such a thing as women's intuition," or a "Mother just knows when her child is in danger."

All these people and many more trust their intuition.

So, what exactly is intuition? For the purposes of this introduction, I interpret it as information flowing toward you. It is not visible or audible. But remember, it can be felt!

We have all experienced receiving intuition by way of a gut feeling, a hunch, a knowing without understanding why we know. Some common examples are when the hair stands up on the back of your neck, giving you a warning. Or there's an uncomfortable creepy feeling that you can't explain when you're around a certain individual. Another example is the unexplained reason why you're compelled to play a number, which ends up winning. They can come to us in several forms like a flash of an image, as subtle physical sensations, a "knowing" something without knowing how. These I call an Intuitive Footprint.

Intuitive Footprints will be explained in detail and exercises will be provided for you to feel and understand Intuitive Footprints. The best way to explain an Intuitive Footprint is to think of old wives tales, such as itchy ears. Supposedly, if your ears are itching or burning, it means someone is talking about you. There are several other possible meanings for an itchy ear: you're going to kiss a fool, you're going to get into a fight, or you may be annoyed or cursed soon.

The fact that there are different meanings for the same physical sensation supports my contention that Intuitive Footprints are different for each of us.

From where do hunches originate? Some think they come from God, Christ, demons, spirits, guardian angels, deceased loved ones, and a whole variety of entities beyond our physical realm.

Now remember this! The goal is to only welcome and trust the information that comes from your highest knowing of God. Knowing this, makes it imperative that you learn to summon it from a strong spiritual foundation to avoid the pitfalls discussed in my book, *The Spiritual Psychic: 4 Necessary Steps for Healers and Light Workers to Protect Against Evil and Demons.* Supportive Godly spiritual forces can maneuver and manipulate situations to try and move you in directions that will best serve you or others. While non-Godly spiritual forces will try to move you in directions that will eventually harm you and others.

Remember the old cartoons, in which a good angel sat on one shoulder of the character and an evil one on the other shoulder? Those cartoons are a great way to picture inspiration and intuition coming to us. But they also serve to warn us, beware of the source from where the information comes.

For most of us, hunches come only occasionally, often suddenly. If you knew where hunches come from, then you can easily call one up on demand. This book will take you through all the steps necessary to be able to call on intuition and be secure about the source of the information, making sure it's coming from God, not demons. It should be mentioned that all the scientists listed above had a strong faith in a Godhead.

Why would you act on a hunch or respond to an intuition? You could use it to decide on the best asking price for your home, and whether to accept the offer you've received. You could use it to decide which automobile on the lot will be the best price and serve your needs. You could use it to even decide what vitamin is best for your child out of the dozens on the drug store shelf.

You could even use it to find your lost dog. I will explain how I did this to find my dog.

This book's purpose is to make available to everyone the ability to accurately and effectively access their inner-net of intuition. We were designed to be more than muscle and bones. We are energy beings. We learn to read the energies surrounding us, and we learn to tap into those energies. We can gain valuable information. Intuition masters and reads these unseen energies. But you must first know how to ask a question to receive an answer. This book will teach you several methods and, most importantly, in a way that is safe from unseen forces whose intentions are to harm you.

There are good and evil forces. The goal is to work strictly with the good, God.

This material will cover several steps. Once learned, they will be second nature to you. When you first learned to ride a bicycle, it took a while to get the concept of balance. But even if you're not on a bike for 20 years you can still find balance the moment you sit on one. It's the same with intuition; once you learn the basics, they never leave you. In fact, what I've seen with many students is that the more they use their intuition and exercise their intuitive muscle, the faster and better it performs.

The speed by which your intuition improves is exponential. A person can learn to play the piano. But it's only after many hours of practice over several years that they really master the piano; this is linear learning.

While intuition is exponential learning, it can grow on itself at speeds that can overwhelm an unprepared person, opening the door to possible dangers.

The following lessons will open a world of information and resources from beyond in amounts that are digestible, limited only by your imagination. They are broken into two major sections: Section A - "Mastering the Basics" and Section B - "Hands On." Section A must be done and mastered before attempting to do any of the exercises in Section B. You can read ahead to Section B, but I strongly recommend that you don't attempt the exercises till you have completed Section A. This is really important to insure that the hunches, intuition, messages are coming from a good source, such as your guardian angel versus the evil ones in disguise. Read through all of the second section before starting any of the exercises.

Section A

Mastering the Basics

In this section we cover four areas: 1) feeling subtle energies with grace and ease, 2) understanding your own energies, 3) understanding why strong spiritual discipline is necessary during this process, and 4) learning how energy flows throughout the physical body systems so as to correctly interpret what's being sensed.

Begin by making a list of people, situations, or circumstances that give you uncomfortable feelings. This will give you a starting point when we dive into the Intuitive Footprint exercises. Finally, your belief that you can trust your intuition will affect your success. So repeat to yourself often, "I trust my intuition."

Chapter 1

Relax, Step Back ™

For thousands of years, Hindus and Buddhist mystics have believed that there is one energy in the universe and that the universe and everything in it vibrates with this energy. This is similar to string theory in physics, in which everything is made up of one-dimensional strings, which are all vibrating. These mystics understood everything is made of the same substance, just as today's physicists believe. This energy, this principle is sometimes described as Omnipresence, prana, chi, or God.

So whether you think like a mystic or like a modern-day physicist, the conclusion is the same; everything in the infinity of space and the eternity of time exists inside of energy that's vibrating. To train yourself to feel this subtle vibration and identify what it's saying is to have accessed your intuitive inner-net on demand. Before you can train yourself to know what the energy is saying, you must first be able to feel it.

There's really only one way to feel subtle energy, and that's through "intuitive relaxation," a relaxed concentrated state. You don't need to be meditating; in fact, you can be driving, having dinner with friends, or watching TV. With the proper amount of discipline and commitment, you can train yourself to step back into the necessary concentrated state of relaxation anytime instantly. I've combined several methods, but must credit *Superlearning* by Sheila Ostrander and Lynn Schroeder (1979) with the bulk of this exercise. I've reduced some of their steps. It's a powerful tool to be used in successfully getting into the intuitive relaxation necessary to read the subtle energies around us.

I call my version the "Relax, Step Back" exercise, which, once mastered, will immediately put your body and mind into the intuitive focused relax stage. This exercise is autogenic, meaning it will require your active involvement in controlling physiological variables in your body. You can expect a marked decrease in stress and tiredness almost immediately, a bonus you could say. It will take 24 days to train your body to enter this autogenic state quickly and with ease. But once learned, you only need to use it a few times a week for a few moments to keep this perfect state of relaxation sharp, which is the key to receiving intuitive information on demand.

These exercises work to master your breathing rhythms and allow you to focus like a laser on any part of your body instantly. The suggestions you give yourself during these exercises are designed to give you the ability to drop into this Relax, Step Back state of mind instantly. Intuition on demand requires this ability to be fully relaxed, while having a sharp attention on the energies around you. The bonus of feeling rested and refreshed makes the time required to learn the process worth every second.

It is imperative to do the work if you wish to reap the rewards. A farmer doesn't throw a few seeds on the ground and expect to yield a bounty. It is only after tilling, sowing, fertilizing, watering, and caring for his fields for months does the bounty come forth. In this case, instead of months and hours of daily labor, it's only 24 days and 20 minutes of relaxation daily. You can practice doing these exercises as often as you wish every day, several times a day even. Just be sure to do them for a full 24 days.

To enter this state of intuitive relaxation on demand, you begin by training your mind to respond to the words *Relax, Step Back* when recited mentally to yourself. The objective of this exercise is to instantly place you in a state of heightened sensitivity, so you can distinguish what energies are around you. While in the relaxed, step back mental state, there's nothing to be achieved; it's a state of witnessing. Later in the book, we will use this Relax, Step Back approach to distinguish what energies are around you, and how to interpret these energies.

Once mastered, you'll have the ability to focus with laser-sharp accuracy on a specific mission, a specific target, while keeping your mind clear. This clarity of mind allows your attention to absorb what's being received. This will enhance your intuition on demand abilities as much as a telescope enhances our ability to explore the stars.

You will learn to be mindful. Instead of using words to describe what you're experiencing, you focus on the physical experiences, what you're feeling in the present moment. The next time you're typing on a computer, driving, or taking a walk, be mindful and feel the experience; avoid using words, and just feel. In the meditation chapter, this topic will be expressed further.

The entire Relax, Step Back, process will take 24 days to complete. You're training your mind to be laser focused and your body to be in an awakened alert state and open to subtle energies during this exercise. Read this completely a few times, before starting it for the first time.

INTUITIVE RELAXATION EXERCISE ONE: RELAX, STEP BACK

Each of these daily exercises will take only 7 to 10 minutes. Done twice a day, it is less than half an hour daily to have the necessary foundation to build your intuition to the level where you can use it on demand. If you choose to do it more than twice a day, it will deepen your skills. It may be tempting to merge a couple of days' worth of exercises together, to move through the process quickly, don't do it. It is imperative that each day's exercise stands alone, giving you time to absorb and master relaxing on demand.

While doing the breathing warm-up, I would suggest using a metronome to help you keep the same timing between counts. It saves you from losing attention because your mind will not have to focus on the time between the counts. There are free metronome apps, so no need to purchase this piece of equipment.

THE WARM-UP EXERCISE:

This daily warm-up exercise will take 2 or 3 minutes. This cannot be skipped and is part of the daily exercises. Don't be fooled by the term *warm-up;* it's not optional, this is an intricate part of the exercise. Set the metronome between 65 and 70 BPM.

Start the metronome. Get into a comfortable position, sitting, lying, or reclining. Relax your face. Say to yourself, "I invite all the muscles in my face, head, and neck to relax." Inviting yourself to relax, instead of telling yourself to relax, helps your mind to avoid thinking of this exercise as work, thus defeating its purpose. Close your eyelids, if they are not already, let your jaw hang loosely with your mouth slightly open. Feel your tongue relax and move it to touch the gum line of your upper teeth. This will prevent you from getting a dry mouth while doing the breathing portion of the exercise. It will take about one minute to do this part of the process up to this point.

Next start a gentle relaxed cycle of deep breathing, don't strain. As you breath in, feel your abdomen puff out. As you exhale, feel your abdomen sink in. Breathe steady. The goal is have your abdomen filled totally with air right at the end of the inhalation count. So by count two, then three, etc. your abdomen is filled. Then expel all air with each exhale exactly by the end of the count. Exhale twice as long as you inhale, increasing the duration with each breath. Allow the metronome to do your timing between counts. The words *In,* representing inhaling, and Out, representing exhale, below are italicized because they are being considered in your count as number one.

You will be breathing in quickly to fill your abdomen fully by the end of each inhalation count in the beginning. It will take practice to be able to breathe in quickly enough when you only have two counts. It will also be just as difficult to breath out slowly not to run out of air before reaching twelve on the last exhalation count. But with practice, it will get easier and you'll begin to control your breathing within the exercise parameters.

In, two; *out* two, three, four
In, two, three; *out* two, three, four, five, six
In, two, three, four; *out* two, three, four, five, six, seven, eight
In, two, three, four, five; *out* two, three, four, five, six, seven, eight, nine, ten
In, two, three, four, five, six; *out* two, three, four, five, six, seven, eight, nine, ten, eleven, twelve

Be aware that you'll be breathing in much slower by the time you get to count six, than you were breathing in at the two count.

Now reverse the cycle starting at six and working back down.
In, two, three, four, five, six; *out* two, three, four, five, six, seven, eight, nine, ten, eleven, twelve
In, two, three, four, five; *out* two, three, four, five, six, seven, eight, nine, ten
In, two, three, four; *out* two, three, four, five, six, seven, eight
In, two, three; *out* two, three, four, five, six
In, two; *out* two, three, four

This completes the warm-up period. Again, the entire warm-up should only be 2 or 3 minutes. You'll repeat this warm-up before you do each of the following sets below. It may be helpful to leave the metronome on, given you'll be doing the warm-up again, before completing the final section.

This appears easy when reading, but don't underestimate the focus and patience you'll need to do this successfully. Don't be harsh with yourself; have a playful heart, even when you stumble. Eventually, it will be as easy to do as it is to read. Given the amount of air you're moving, expect to be lightheaded the first few times you do the warm-up.

You'll need to use your imagination in the next part. Imagination is the key that unlocks the door to these unseen forces surrounding us and our world. Think what Albert Einstein said about imagination: "When I examine myself and my methods of thought, I come close to the conclusion that the gift of imagination has meant more to me than any talent for absorbing absolute knowledge." Be imaginative, be gentle with yourself, be playful like a child.

The Relax, Step Back

Do each section twice daily, preferable within 6 hours of the first session. Each section below starts with the above warm-up. You'll do the same section for 3 days before moving to the next section. During each session, you'll do the exercise twice. Basically, in the morning for session one, do warm-up above followed by section one below then repeat these two steps. That completes the morning session. You'll do the same process for the afternoon session. After 3 days, you'll do the same process, moving to the next section.

If you wish to practice more often, go ahead. Just do the first session when you wake up, second before dinner, and last before going to sleep. Do your best to have the first and last daily practice session at least eight hours apart. A reasonable amount of time between sessions is important.

Days 1-3

Start with Warm-Up Exercise

Section 1: Silently, with intention, repeat the following to yourself. Use your imagination to feel these repeated commands working.

My arms are getting limp, heavy, and warm	repeat 6-8 times
My arms are getting heavier and warmer	repeat 6-8 times
My arms are completely relaxed and warm	repeat 6-8 times
I feel completely calm and alert	state 1 time
I easily and naturally sense subtle energies	state 1 time
I enter this state anytime by telling myself:	
"Relax, Step Back"	state 1 time

Repeat warm-up exercise

Repeat section 1

Days 4-6

Start with Warm-Up Exercise

Section 2: Silently, with intention repeat the following to yourself. Use your imagination to feel these repeated commands working.

My arms are completely relaxed and warm	state 1 time
My legs are getting limp, heavy, and warm	repeat 6-8 times
My legs are getting heavier and warmer	repeat 6-8 times
My legs are completely relaxed and warm	repeat 6-8 times
I feel completely calm and alert	state 1 time
I easily and naturally sense subtle energies	state 1 time
I enter this state anytime by telling myself	
"Relax, Step Back"	state 1 time

Repeat warm-up exercise

Repeat section 2

Days 7-9

Start with Warm-Up Exercise

Section 3: Silently, with intention repeat the following to yourself. Use your imagination to feel these repeated commands working.

My arms and legs are getting limp, heavy, and warm	repeat 6-8 times
My arms and legs are getting heavier and warmer	repeat 6-8 times
My arms and legs are completely relaxed and warm	repeat 6-8 times
I feel completely calm and alert	state 1 time
I easily and naturally sense subtle energies	state 1 time
I enter this state anytime by telling myself "Relax, Step Back"	state 1 time

Repeat warm-up exercise

Repeat section 3

Days 10-12

Start with Warm-Up Exercise

Section 4: Silently, with intention repeat the following to yourself. Use your imagination to feel these repeated commands working.

My arms and legs are getting limp, heavy, and warm	state 1 time
My arms and legs are completely heavy and warm	state 1 time
My chest feels warm and pleasant	repeat 6-8 times
My heartbeat is calm and steady	repeat 6-8 times
I feel completely calm and alert	state 1 time
I easily and naturally sense subtle energies	state 1 time
I enter this state anytime by telling myself "Relax, Step Back"	state 1 time

Repeat warm-up exercise

Repeat section 4

Days 13-15

Start with Warm-Up Exercise

Section 5: Silently, with intention repeat the following to yourself. Use your imagination to feel these repeated commands working.

My arms and legs are relaxed and warm	state 1 time
My chest feels warm and pleasant	state 1 time
My heartbeat is calm and steady	state 1 time
My breathing is supremely calm	repeat 6-8 times
I feel completely calm and alert	state 1 time
I easily and naturally sense subtle energies	state 1 time
I enter this state anytime by telling myself "Relax, Step Back"	state 1 time

Repeat warm-up exercise

Repeat section 5

Days 16-18

Start with Warm-Up Exercise

Section 6: Silently, with intention repeat the following to yourself. Use your imagination to feel these repeated commands working.

My arms and legs are relaxed and warm	state 1 time
My chest feels warm and pleasant	state 1 time
My heartbeat and breath are calm and steady	state 1 time
My stomach is getting soft and warm	repeat 6-8 times

My stomach is soft and warm	repeat 6-8 times
I feel completely calm and alert	state 1 time
I easily and naturally sense subtle energies	state 1 time
I enter this state anytime by telling myself	
"Relax, Step Back"	state 1 time

Repeat warm-up exercise

Repeat section 6

Days 19-21

Start with Warm-Up Exercise

Section 7: Silently, with intention repeat the following to yourself. Use your imagination to feel these repeated commands working.

My arms and legs are relaxed and warm	state 1 time
My chest feels warm and pleasant	state 1 time
My heartbeat and breath are calm and steady	state 1 time
My stomach is soft and warm	state 1 time
My forehead is cool	repeat 6-8 times
I feel completely calm and alert	state 1 time
I easily and naturally sense subtle energies	state 1 time
I enter this state anytime by telling myself	
"Relax, Step Back"	state 1 time

Repeat warm-up exercise

Repeat section 7

Days 22-24

Start with Warm-Up Exercise

Section 8: Silently, with intention, repeat the following to yourself and use your imagination to feel these repeated commands working.

My arms and legs are relaxed and warm	state 1 time
My chest feels warm and pleasant	state 1 time
My heartbeat and breath are calm and steady	state 1 time
My stomach is warm and my forehead is cool	state 1 time
I feel completely calm and alert	state 1 time
I easily and naturally sense subtle energies	state 1 time
I enter this state by anytime telling myself "Relax, Step Back"	state 1 time

Repeat warm-up exercise

Repeat section 8

Upon completing all 24 days of these exercises, you're in control over the rhythm of your breathing and your mind is able to laser-focus on any part of your body. Your suggestions opened your mind to accepting its natural ability to sense energies. You also trained yourself to go into this state of laser-focused attention while being relaxed simply by suggesting "Relax, Step Back" to yourself. This will be the foundation of many of the following exercises. Intuition on demand requires the ability to relax while having a sharp attention, not a sleepy state; it's an ability to laser-focus on demand. You now have trained yourself to accomplish this.

Each of these daily exercises will take only 7 to 10 minutes. Done twice a day is less than half an hour daily to have the necessary foundation to build your intuition to the level where you can use it on demand.

It is helpful to occasional repeat warm-up and section 8 exercise once a month just to keep the muscle of relaxed intuition toned. In Section B, you'll be telling yourself to "Relax, Step Back" to begin most exercises.

It is imperative to have done this section thoroughly if you expect accurate intuition on demand. It cannot be emphasized enough; this one exercise will change your life when it comes to enhancing your intuition.

The additional benefit, not related to intuition, is that Relax, Step Back will enhance your decision-making skills because a relaxed mind thinks more clearly.

Often, students ask how I know when energy is present that's not being created by me. The only way to distinguish another's energy from your own is to know your own energy as well as you know your image in a mirror. We can do this by working with Energy Balls.

Chapter 2

Energy Ball

This chapter focuses on understanding your own energy so well that you can easily pick up another energy that's different. This section can be practiced simultaneously with the "Relax, Step Back" exercises. You don't need to complete all 24 days before beginning this process.

Before you can learn to read other energies, you want to know what your energy is like. Imagine your energy to be the foundation wall of your body. All your energy systems are attached to your foundation wall. If suddenly you're feeling overwhelmed, you can check on your foundation wall and sense if there's something wrong within your field or if you're picking it up from someone else. This is extremely important because the more sensitive you become to your intuition, the more empathic you become. Being empathic has its benefits as well as challenges, which we will cover in a later chapter.

To understand your energy foundation, make an energy ball every hour, every day for one month. The exact steps to making an energy ball will take a large commitment on your part. Some of you may not be able to stop doing what you're doing every hour to test your energy, especially when at work. Do it as often as possible, and every hour on your days off. After recording the information you experience for one month in the Energy Ball Table in Appendix G, you'll know with sufficient certainty your personal patterns.

First, how do you make an energy ball?

You can be sitting or standing. For the purposes of learning about yourself, it doesn't matter which position you chose, or if you change that position on different days. Both feet need to be on the floor, to allow for a good connection. I call this grounding. Tell yourself "Relax, Step Back," even if you're not done working on the Relax, Step Back exercise. It's still helpful to start using it. Put your laser-sharp attention into your hands and notice the energy radiating from your palms. Bring your hands in front of you with the palms facing each other. Stay focused on the subtle energy between your hands. The more you practice the Relax, Step Back exercise, the more laser sharp your attention will become, and the more you'll feel the energy.

There is a school of thought to rub your palms together before focusing on the energy between the palms. I found that students often don't believe they're feeling energy but, instead, are feeling the effects of the hands being rubbed together. For this reason, I don't encourage you to rub your hands together. Energy is there; simply bring your laser-sharp attention to it, and you'll feel it.

Imagination will help you start the engine. If you don't feel anything between your hands, imagine you do. Imagine heat. Imagine a pushing or pulling sensation. Move your hands toward each other and away and imagine the energy feeling like a rubber band. Within moments, if you allow your imagination to turn the key of your intuitive engine, you'll be feeling it, not just imagining it.

While your hands are feeling the energy, play with it. Bring your palms closer together, pull them apart, and see how far apart you can get your hands without losing contact with the energy ball. Mentally note the frequency, the number of times you sense the energy moving from one hand to the next. Mentally note the strength on a scale of 1 to 10. Mentally question if there is heat, coolness, or something in between. Note if there's an invisible pressure pushing your hands apart, or together, or not at all. Note, the location energy emanates from, fingertips, whole finger, palms, or fingers and palms. Do this for 1 to 3 minutes. Lastly, notice the mood you're in, calm, anxious, feeling silly, tense, nervous, etc.

Use the Energy Ball Table in Appendix G to chart your impressions for one day. Make copies of this form to chart your results for one month.

Even if you never intend to use intuition, or call for a hunch on demand, knowing your own personal energy patterns, allows you to make better decisions. Making major decisions is best done when your energy is on the upswing. If you need to have a serious conversation with someone, it's best done when your energy is on its upswing. You'll know when it's on its upswing by seeing in the charts what time of day your energy was reading was strongest, most frequent, etc.

According to Mietek Wirkus, a world renowned bioenergy healer from Poland, our energy patterns never change, even when we're sick. So once you know when your energy is highest, or climbing, you can schedule that time of day for your most important decision making and your lower energy time for relaxing.

Now that you have survived the two most difficult chapters, the rest is as easy as pie. There are three foundations needed for accurate interpretation of intuition.

First, the Relax, Step Back exercise, which we will continue to use throughout the book to assist you in easily accessing your laser focus, to pick up on the energies surrounding a situation.

The second foundation is the energy ball exercise. In addition to the benefit of understanding your own energies, it provides a platform for interpreting the energies you're picking up around yourself or a situation.

The third and most important foundation is the spiritual component, which is necessary both to protect yourself and to avoid receiving poor information.

Chapter 3

Power of Prayer:
Spirituality as Protection

Your personal spiritual life is key to insuring that the intuition and hunches you receive are coming from your highest best source, God. Spiritual life without discipline is basically a cork floating in the ocean. Discipline builds the ship needed to weather a storm. One discipline at a time. Honoring the Sabbath builds the hull, fasting builds the rudder, submission builds the sails, and so forth. Until you've built a spiritual ship that can weather the storms evil throws your way, it's best to not delve into the intuitive world of hunches. With a strong spiritual discipline, your hunches and intuition will direct you through all of life's storms.

Often, one of my spiritual prayer partners and I are called to help those who are experiencing extremely bizarre paranormal activity in their homes. The second most common call we receive is about types of possession, attachments, and/or harassment. We've asked ourselves often why people don't understand how to pray and protect themselves, and end up needing our intervention. What we found is troubling; most people see Satan as mythology and not reality.

New Testament writers testified to Satan's rule on earth. His minions, the other fallen angels, demons, assist him. In a passage where the devil tempts Jesus, the Devil declares he has authority over "all the kingdoms of the world" (Luke 4:5-6). Paul, throughout Corinthians, makes it clear that the world was subjugated to Satan or evil powers, while John's gospel considers Satan "the ruler of this world" (John 12:31; 14:30). There are close to a hundred New Testament reference of Jesus' casting out demons. So why do people continue to believe that Satan, the Evil One, is at best mythology or folklore? Why do they not teach each other and their children the proper way to protect ourselves from this evil? And why am I bringing it up in this book?

Unfortunately, those who consider themselves rational and scientific just don't believe in the Devil anymore. However, you risk all when you're indifferent to the existence of evil and dive into a world of unseen forces such as intuition. The greatest accomplishment of the Devil is convincing reasonable minded people that he doesn't exist. This grants evil the ability to move undetected. It is human nature to pride ourselves on being enlightened. We do everything possible to convince ourselves we are right. What's more disturbing than ignoring evil is glamorizing it. Young people are captivated by Hollywood and other media creations that portray evil energy as romantic. *True Blood, Twilight,* and *Da Vinci's Demons* to name a few, really push home the belief that evil is romantic and sexually desirable, playing on basic human desires.

Even more frightening than the romanticizing of evil is its infiltration of our churches. Exorcist, scholar, Vatican insider, and best-selling author, Father Malachi Martin, in his book *Hostage to the Devil,* states, "In at least three major cities, members of the clergy have at their disposal at least one pedophiliac coven peopled and maintained exclusively by and for the clergy."

In *The Fatima Crusader* Father Martin, said, "Anybody who is acquainted with the state of affairs in the last 35 years is well aware that the prince of darkness has had and still has his surrogates in the court of St. Peter in Rome." Sadly, the infiltration into the church has been expanding since 1961 or shortly before the death of Pope John XXIII.

I'm not implying that everything out of Hollywood is evil and glorifies evil; but to assume these productions are harmless romantic stories is seriously dangerous. Nor is it my intention to say all the Catholic Church is evil. Far from it, it is loaded with good and holy people. My intent is to make you aware of the need to pray and have a spiritual discipline. The devil is not under every rock, but he is under enough to warrant this warning and the need to cultivate spiritual protection.

When we start using intuition on demand, a sound way to be sure you're not being influenced by demons is to have a strong spiritual discipline. You can't be an occasionally prayerful person. Working with subtle energies, we can easily be misguided if our foundations are built on sand and not rock. Having personally seen the trouble in which so many people find themselves, and the ease with which they can avoid such turmoil, makes it necessary for me to stand on a soap box and yell, "PRAY!" In my book, *The Spiritual Psychic: 4 Necessary Steps for Healers and Light Workers to Protect Against Evil and Demons,* I've shared only a few of the very frightening situations people who are not spiritual get into.

Say the Lord's Prayer (Appendix A) before starting your day. Ask for God's Divine Love to shine upon you and your family, protecting and nurturing all of you. The apostle Peter warns us to "Be sober-minded; be watchful. Your adversary the devil prowls around like a roaring lion, seeking someone to devour." Let prayer protect you. The St. Michael the Archangel prayer (Appendix B) is one anyone would benefit from if said daily. Both these prayers will not only protect you but also insure the intuition you're calling upon is coming from a divine source that wants to nurture and care for you.

So far, we've learned three important exercises, all foundation builders: Relax, Step Back; energy balls, to learn about your own energy; and the necessity of prayer. These are the three basic principles for strong intuitive skills. Now we have one basic piece left before stitching these all together into workable experiences: understanding the body's energy systems.

Chapter 4

Elementary Understanding of the Body's Energy Systems

Let's begin by defining the often-used word *energy,* which has been broadly used to describe so many areas of our bodies and lives. We need to agree on what's meant by energy for the purposes of our discussion. We need to understand that all living things, including us, are composed of energy, and when it's not present, as confirmed by an EEG or EKG, we are dead according to medical science. This energy of the body's energy systems is often referred to as the soul, which animates life.

With that said, you need to understand there is an energy that permeates all things, even nonliving, and that energy is also what we will be reading when we cover psychometry.

All living organisms are surrounded by an energy, a universal force that animates matter. Although every living organism has its own individual energy print, this energy mingles, merges, and dances with the energy of all the other living organisms around it continuously. All matter is awash in this field of universal energy, and becoming more aware of this energy allows us to understand how to call on intuition and hunches more fully.

Have you ever noticed, when you meet someone for the first time, you're either comfortable with them or not? You're sensing their energy fields.

Energy is intricately interwoven within itself to form our bodies. Our bodies emit energy, which is picked up by others as intuition. We are always sending messages out to others energetically. In addition, our bodies are pulling in energy and we are receiving intuitive information from the universal energy field and from others around us.

Each of us has three energy fields that surround our bodies. With practice, we can move into more complex forms of intuition beyond hunches such as medical intuition. Since part of this book will touch on medical intuition and reading auras, it's best to take some time to study the three energy fields surrounding our bodies and the corresponding chakras, which are part of our energy system.

The first energy field radiating from the body is the etheric field. This energy only radiates between two and three inches from a healthy person. It provides information on a person's physical health and vitality. All living organisms have this etheric energy field surrounding them. It is often referred to as the matrix of the physical body because it provides the information about the energy flow for all the internal parts of our body.

When you're sick, this field pulls in closer to your body. The etheric field is reminiscent to being tucked in by your loving parent when you were a child. This field wraps you more tightly to keep you well protected when you're ill. At those times, it's hard to see because it pulls in to within an inch of the person's physical body, making detection with your eyes more difficult. It appears more like a line outlining the body when a person is sick, then a shadow surrounding the body when a person is healthy. More on this in the chapter on seeing auras.

These three fields work in conjunction with chakras to deliver universal energy into our individual fields and into our bodies. Each chakra in the etheric field is linked to a particular organ and a particular gland's function. (See Appendix C) The etheric field transfers the universal energy from the chakras, allowing it to distribute this nourishing, nurturing energy into the organs and gland systems. In the chapter on medical intuition, we will understand the importance of knowing which chakras feed energy into which gland and organ.

The second energy field is called by many names, the astral body, the electromagnetic field, the emotional field, and aura. This field energy is more mobile and runs at a higher frequency than it does in the etheric field. The astral field is my personal favorite to work with, because it provides us with warnings, gut feelings, and hunches.

This field of energy is the curious field. It moves quickly to investigate everything and everyone around us. How often do you say to someone, "I was just thinking of you" when they called? It's the field that feeds us the information about this person, because it's exploring what's occurring around us all the time, with very little limits. The chakras in this field align with specific emotions (See Appendix C).

The third energy field is the mental body, which connects us to our highest source of Universal Energy. Its main chakra is the "third eye." As we develop it, we naturally become more aware of the subtle energies. We realize then that we are only a small part of the greater whole, Omnipotent God. This mental level is the highest level one person can operate when helping another.

The mental body's frequency is much higher than the astral level. When a person changes the way they look at others, and the events in their life, this part of the energy field is affected. If the change is positively uplifting, the energy fields receive new vibrations in the emotional body, influencing the energy on the etheric level, which subsequently improves the energy flows in the physical body.

In the mental field, thoughts create our realities. Thus, it's important to be aware of the thoughts you dwell on. In Genesis, we read how God spoke everything into existence. When God created us in his image and likeness, this image and likeness has the ability to speak things into existence, from its own mental field. If a car speeds by cutting us off, for many, the first instinct is to curse at the person. By doing this, we've added to the chaos of the world, we've added the emotion of anger into the universal field. Often, the result you get is more and more drivers cutting you off, because you're emitting anger and aggression. You have attracted anger and aggression. In addition, the sharing of oneself, giving love freely, will not only improve the overall health of the one receiving it, but also the one giving it. Pray for the driver.

Jesus said to pray without ceasing. This is an excellent way to protect ourselves from the careless wandering of the mind, which can create chaos in this field. If our thoughts are continuously on prayer and thanksgiving, we are creating in this mental body harmony and peace. Notice the next time someone cuts you off, or does something else that causes you to become angry without thinking. In that instant, say a quick prayer for the person. Let the anger go by asking God to protect them and all those around him/her. You now have released loving understanding into the world, resulting in your experiencing more peaceful drivers around you in general.

Instead of putting anger into the universal field through your mental/emotional field, you put loving prayer and thought. You have just healed the world a little. If you do this enough, there will be fewer times said instances arise that cause you to become angry, because like attracts like, and you're not calling forth anger but peace through prayer.

The exchange of energies between these three fields is a natural process. One change in vibration and flow in any field will affect the other two instantly. These positive loving thoughts were generated from the mental body of the giver, so the giver's etheric and astral energies bodies are instantly positively affected as well as the receiver of the prayer. Next the positive loving thoughts now move into the chakras that feed the physical body. So the loving thoughts, or energies, are feeding the giver's body just as much as the receiver's body. As mentioned previously, the same is true with negative hurtful thoughts; the senders are harming their own body as much as they intend to harm another with their thoughts.

There are two different schools on the flow of energy through the chakras, both covered in *The Spiritual Psychic: 4 Necessary Steps for Healers and Light Workers to Protect Against Evil and Demons.* For the purposes of this book, it does not matter. I listed them in the order I personally sense energy flowing. The colors that traditional correspond to these chakras are symbolic and not necessarily what you'll see when you practice the medical intuitive chapter.

Below is a sketch of where the chakras aligned with the physical body. But the chakras are not just in the body; these energy-spinning systems that feed our physical body expand out into the three energy fields surrounding our physical body.

Now you have a basic understanding of the energy systems that will be used to assist you in creating hunches and calling upon your intuition in Section B. You have taken the time and practiced the steps to build upon from this point forward. Before jumping in feet first, we need to look at the stumbling blocks to successfully calling on hunches.

Chapter 5

The Dreaded Stumbling Blocks

Our feet were once stumbling blocks to learning how to walk; now, we just rely on them without thought. Intuition and hunches are no different. Stumbling blocks are everywhere whenever we take on something new. Stumbling blocks are not bad. They present opportunities to learn how to convert stumbling blocks into building blocks. There are standard stumbling blocks we all face, but once we overcome them, these blocks actually become foundation stones to our success.

Tension, past beliefs, and intelligence are the three biggest stumbling blocks to calling for a hunch on demand.

Tension is often caused by our desire to be successful, so we have performance anxiety, even though the only person we are performing for is our self. Of course, let's not forget that we are our own worst critic, so the tension to be good at something can be pretty high. Now the good news is that tension can be helpful. It can act as a reminder to use the statement Relax, Step Back, instantly pulling you into the state of laser sharp concentration and full relaxation to be successful at interpreting the energy. So as soon as your mind wanders, or your muscles tense, be grateful for the physical signs letting you know your tension is interfering and apply Relax, Step Back.

The next stumbling block is our past beliefs. For most of us, nobody in our past told us it's possible to have a hunch on demand or that it's effective to use our intuition when making important decisions in our lives. Probably the opposite happened to you; you were encouraged to get your head out of the clouds and focus on the here and now. That wasn't really bad advice because you need to be out of your head and fully present to the here and now to be successful at intuition. As you call on our intuition, you'll learn there are specific steps to getting an answer, none of which require you to have your head in the clouds. If you start to think of old beliefs, just be present, Relax, Step Back.

Now meet a real stumbling block, our intelligence. When our intelligence steps in to act as a stumbling block, it usually shows up as doubt. Your intuition brings a result but thoughts arise such as "This can't be real," "I just made that up," or "It's my imagination." Albert Einstein's famous quote sums up why this is a foundation stone, not a stumbling block. "Imagination is more important than knowledge. For knowledge is limited to all we now know and understand, while imagination embraces the entire world and all there ever will be to know and understand."

When "This is just my imagination" thoughts start, think of the mental energy body, and say to yourself, "Yes! My imagination will turn the key to unlock this door so I can embrace the entire world. Einstein would be proud of me." This positive affirmation about imagination, will move your energy forward to reach into those areas were hunches wait to be received.

You now have all the basics. You have enough understanding about our energy fields and blocks. You understand the three foundations. You find your mind and body relaxing and being laser-focused simply by stating,

"Relax, Step Back." You tracked your own energy using energy balls to establish your personal peaks and valleys while becoming personally familiar with your own energy. Third, you understand the importance of spiritual practices.

If you did your homework, good job. We can now play. If not, you'll miss much of what we are about to do.

Section B

Hands On

The key to understanding and learning to master intuition is being able to identify subtle energy on your own body and interpret these energies, a technique I call finding the "Intuitive Footprint." These chapters will build upon what you have already learned. Using the Relax, Step Back approach, in conjunction with sensing energy balls gives you the foundation to opening an entire new world of understand your surroundings.

Now it's time to tap into your intuition.

There are three simple steps you need to do every time you want information intuitively. First, tell yourself to "Relax, Step Back." Your mind is trained from the previous work, to immediately put you into a relaxed state. Your laser-focused attention is ready to be assigned a task. Next, you assign a task by asking your question. Asking a question is how you direct the laser-focused attention. Lastly, receive the information. Receiving the information can come in several forms depending on the method you're using to receive the information. Each of these steps will be discussed for every type of intuitive retrieval method explained.

Let's be clear on the proper way to ask a question.

Simply, in your mind, state your question. That's it. Let's look at how to word questions to be beneficial and not misleading.

Sarah might ask, "Will I marry Bobby?" The answer may be a very clear "Yes," but is that the right question. What if Sarah then marries Bobby only to find out he's abusive and violent. The best way for Sarah to ask this question is, "If I choose to marry Bobby, will I experience the type of joy and happiness I wish to experience in a marriage?" Or "Is Bobby the person God chose for me to marry in order to learn and grow through life with?"

It is wise to word your questions with Divine purpose. For example, "Is it God's will that I marry Bobby?" The answer of yes or no does not guaranteeing an easy road; it's just confirming or denying God's will in that situation. It's easy to be misguided with answers, when the questions are profound, coming from a deep place of desire. I will address how to avoid this in Chapter 7, Trusting Your Mind.

You become better with experience. Think out your questions carefully. I still laugh at how poorly I structured questions especially when I want to hurry up and get some advice. Not too long ago I needed a printer for my office. I stated in my mind, Relax, Step Back. Then I asked where I would find the particular model printer I want for an excellent price. I received the image immediately of one of the smaller malls not far from my home. As I walked through the mall, I saw the printer on display and sure enough, the price was right. However, after purchasing it, I saw the same printer, in another store, for slightly less.

In asking my question about the printer, I should have followed up with the name or location of the store within the mall. Sometimes, even I get giddy when I receive answers so easily. Occasionally, even I forget to be sure there's no further information available, or to be sure I'm asking my questions in a way to insure I don't get mislead.

Chapter 6

Retrieving the Intuitive Information

What was that causing your hair to stand on edge? What was the unexplained chill down your spine? What was that which made you not want to go into the car and avoid an accident?

All the work you did in the previous chapters is now going to be used so you can answer these questions.

This next exercise will again take time to fully understand. The more effort you put into discovering how your body senses energy, the more information you'll interpret correctly. Information is freely flowing to you even as you read this. Now you'll tap into that information and use it in decision making.

Make several copies of this outline of a body image, in appendix D. You want to label several of these images with different emotions. Label them as follows: Joy, Kindness, Gratitude, Anger, and Frustration.

Now the fun begins. We are going to use a method I call "Intuitive Footprint." Start by noticing a certain type of emotion that may be present in you. For example, let's suppose that gratefulness is the emotion present. Imagine that you're witnessing your niece opening a gift that she really needed, and she is expressing her gratefulness. It is important to remember that you're not to be in the emotion, but just be a witness to the emotion. While being a witness to this emotion, actively pay attention to your body, following these steps immediately. You're actively feeling for changes on your body, to identify the Intuitive Footprint.

1. Give yourself the instructions to "Relax, Step Back" As stated earlier, this Relax, Step Back method will bring you into the relaxed state necessary to retrieve intuitive messages, while setting your mind to the single laser focus necessary to complete the task at hand.

2. Ask questions to determine what you feel and where you feel it on your body. Actively scan your body and notice where on your body you feel gratitude when you ask the question. If you're witnessing a different emotion, then you would again ask where on your body that emotion manifests itself.

3. Identify what sensations are present on your body. Ask yourself, Did the temperature on my skin change anywhere? Do I feel pressure, itching, or tingling anywhere on my body? Does it feel like someone is tapping my skin?

4. Locate where you are sensing the sensations on your body such as the bottom of your feet, left nostril, or pinky finger on right hand. We all sense it in different places on our bodies.

Be as specific as possible. For example, in one intuitive flash of sensing gratitude, "intuitive footprint," the bottoms of my feet felt like tingling shots and the sensation moved up to three inches below my knees, causing my legs to feel as if energy were radiating outward in beams no thicker than a strand a hair. This entire sensation lasted for close to 2 minutes.

Once you believe you have it, draw it on the figure labeled "gratitude" and explain exactly what you felt in the space below it. Include the time of day, the situation, and any information you think is relevant to remembering how you felt during the exercise. You now have successful labeled your first "Intuitive Footprint."

Repeat this exercise as often as possible with a different set of circumstances every time you know there's an obvious emotion present. It's important that the emotion be present in the room with other people, not with you. You're just a witness. You must remain neutral to distinguish where the emotion's footprint appears on your body. Eventually, you'll build a large library of intuitive footprints distinct to your body. Do the same emotion several times, testing it to be sure you have the correct footprint, creating affirmation for yourself and confidence in your personal discovery. These Intuitive Footprints only appear during observation of people in real situations. Television and movies will not cause the effect you need, even if the show is based on a true story.

There could be an argument made for using a stage play to identify an intuitive footprint. Performers often relive actual memories that relate to the emotion being portrayed; therefore, the actual energy footprint will be present. But given there is an audience, all experiencing their own emotions and other performers experiencing more emotions, its best to keep training simple. However, for an advanced student who has absolutely identified their emotional footprints, this would make an interesting exercise to see if they could sense emotion of one person in a room filled with so many others.

Look for opportunities to sense an emotion. The next time the customer in line ahead of you is frustrated at the customer representative, there's an excellent opportunity to test frustration. As soon as you're aware that there's definitely an identifiable emotion surfacing, "Relax, Step Back," and, using your laser-sharp attention, notice what's happening on your body. Just your body! Pay no attention to your surroundings. Start from the top of your head and scan your body down to your toes. What's different? Was there a sudden temperature change somewhere on your body? Did you feel an itching sensation, if so where? There are thousands of sensations that can be felt in thousands of ways, but in only one way does subtle energy of frustration shows up on your body in the form of an Intuitive Footprint every time.

One student identified her frustration Intuitive Footprint as her left ear lobe became itchy, another as his right forearm had a flash of heat, and still another as his left bicep felt chilled for a moment. Now, once you believe you have it, draw it on the figure labeled "Frustration" and explain exactly what you felt in the space below it. Include the time of day, the situation, and any information you think is relevant to remembering what you felt during the exercise.

Just as with gratitude, you may or may not have identified how the footprint of frustration will show up on your body. You need to be thorough. You need to notice the next time someone is frustrated near you and, again, immediately "Relax, Step Back" and focus laser sharp attention on your body to scan for subtle energies. Record what your body tells you. Continue to do this for every emotion listed as often as possible.

Within a month, you will have identified several emotions and how the subtle energies of these Intuitive Footprints appear on your body. I've included several of my personal drawings (Appendix E) and notes to assist you in tracking these emotions or subtle energy footprints. The more effort you put into learning to read the Intuitive Footprints of the surrounding subtle energies on your body, the more value you will be for others and yourself.

Intuitive Footprints are as individual as fingerprints. No two people will sense an emotion in the same exact spot in the same exact way. It is important to create your own personal library. There's an exception to this rule. There are a few Intuitive Footprints that are universal. One is the "Don't Do It!" or "Something's Wrong" Intuitive Footprint.

So what? Why do all that work just to know that my legs between my knees and the bottom of my feet may tingle when someone is feeling gratitude? It just seems like an awful lot of work, first the Relax, Step Back exercises a month, tracking my energy ball for a month, now this!?

The best way to explain why doing these exercises is worth all the work is to take the Intuitive Footprint for "Something's Wrong!" also called the "Don't Do It!" Intuitive Footprint, which manifests as a feeling in the pit of our stomachs. When you get this feeling in the pit of your stomach, has it ever steered you wrong? No, it has not! Most likely, it has always been right. Knowing just this one Intuitive Footprint makes a huge difference in your life.

Unfortunately, the "Don't Do It!" "Something's Wrong" Intuitive Footprints are only one of a very few universal footprints. Because most emotions or messages come to each of us in a unique fashion, it requires this study period to understand what energy you're sensing.

We all have different physical signs for different emotions; very few are universal. Because they are not universal, we don't realize their importance and usefulness, like the feeling in the pit of our stomachs. We don't have group consensus, making it easier to understand the usefulness of identifying these subtle energies or Intuitive Footprints. I know of another universal footprint we all have, called "Push back!" I will explain more about this in a later chapter.

Let's review some examples of why knowing what subtle energy is present is helpful. Obviously, you'll be doing this exercise when you know what emotion is present, allowing you to identify its footprint on your body. The eventual purpose being when you don't know what emotion is present, you'll sense it on your body, and know that emotion is present in the other person or the room. You won't see it with your eyes or know it from conversations, but you will feel it.

Often, someone will appear very calm and levelheaded, but if you're sensing sadness on your body, you know the person is really coming from a place a sadness, and you can change your position to better serve that person, such as give the person space they need to deal with their sorrow. If you did not sense the presence of sadness, you would have no idea and would continue dealing with the sad person, thinking they were just not on their game, and you most likely will not show the needed compassion. You may even get angry that the person is not responding appropriately.

Let's say you and a fellow coworker are working on a project. If you're sensing frustration from a fellow coworker, who is not otherwise showing signs of stress or upset, you can steer the conversation in a way to figure out what's frustrating the coworker. Clearing up the frustration will allow you both to be more productive. You may find that something in their home life is frustrating them, and your simple listening helps them deal better with their emotion, making working on the project easier.

Many of us have that one family member who cannot accept a gift graciously. The first thing they ask is what you spent, followed quickly by the statement of how you wasted your money because it's not needed or is too expensive. If your gratitude signals are firing on your body, you know the person is very grateful even if they're not good at expressing it. This reduces the upset that would usually follow the giving of a gift and replaces it with joy. Now you have concrete evidence the gift is appreciated; it's just the person has difficultly expressing it.

As we open our intuition, we want to be sure the messages are coming from a joyful, good place, from God. Many people have claimed to see angelic beings and speak with them, evidence by all the books on angel communication. They say they saw an angelic being, or saw a beautiful light, so they immediately believe the message to be safe and coming from a Godly source. Let's not forget that Lucifer is the Angel of Light, he can disguise himself in light or something else that looks beautiful. So one can easily be fooled by an angelic image, which is really a wolf in sheep's clothing if we trust just the abilities of our five physical senses. Our senses can be deceiving in these situations, making us vulnerable to manipulation.

Demons cannot hide the energy that sources them into existence. This energy is anger. Once you can identify your Intuitive Footprint for anger, you'll not be deceived by evil. No matter how beautiful it may appear, or how peaceful its message, if your anger Intuitive Footprint is triggered, you know that the message is being given by a demon in disguise.

To be able to sense anger is an excellent way to protect oneself from dark forces or simply bad people. Once I was sitting in my favorite prayer and meditation chair, doing some spiritual writing, the messages coming through seems beautiful and peaceful. But suddenly I felt a flash on the left side of my face, which is my personal Intuitive Footprint for how the subtle energy of anger appears on my body. Immediately, I knew that the messages I was receiving were from a demon or evil entity posing as good to fool me into trusting it. If I could not sense the subtle energy of anger being present, I would have easily fallen into a false sense of trust. Knowing the anger Intuitive Footprint protected me. In that moment, I said a prayer, banishing that entity from every interfering with me again.

I know when anger is present; I've trained myself to sense it. I basically set myself up to have on demand the knowledge of anger being present, which protects me from being fooled. It grants me the sense of security, knowing that evil may try to mislead me, but it can't mislead my ability to sense the anger sourcing it, hence, creating a safe environment for myself and those around me. I'm not saying that Satan cannot fool me; I'm not that arrogant. But in the same sense, I'm much safer than 99% of the others who work as psychics, mediums, and channels because I have the knowledge of my Intuitive Footprint for anger.

Often, people who are intuitive suffer from being empathic. Once you can identify the subtle energy as Intuitive Footprints, you realize it's not coming from you, but to you, providing you the option of turning it off. Utilizing this option has helped many empaths I've taught over the years. Many people suffer from anxiety and depression, but don't realize they are picking up other people's subtle energies, causing them to believe they are suddenly depressed, when instead they just passed a stranger who lost a loved one, and now they're feeling that emotion. With the ability to distinguish the emotion as an Intuitive Footprint, you're no longer holding onto the emotion as your own, but understand, instead, that it was something you just passed.

I hope these few examples helped you understand why it's worth taking the time to understand these subtle energies or Intuitive Footprints. You'll find countless ways they serve you once you start to distinguish them for yourself. Many of these methods of understanding and tapping into our intuition take time; others are quick. The next chapter will explain one of the easiest and quickest methods for tapping into your intuition.

Chapter 7

Trusting Your Mind

Earlier, we discussed the three main energy fields surrounding your physical body. The third field was the mental field, that which is closest to the universal field of all energy. From the mental field we can ask almost anything and receive feedback quickly.

There are three steps to remember when asking for intuition from this field. First, Relax, Step Back. By doing this, you immediately put yourself in the mental relax state of focused attention needed to ask a question. I cannot emphasis enough how this simple exercise is the key to calling on intuition in every exercise.

Second, word your question in a simple sentence. You can ask as many questions as you like, just keep each one simple. For example, you might ask, "Should I take that new job across town, and if I do, should I move?" This question leaves the door open for confusion when receiving your intuition. Was the answer for the first part of your question or the second part? Instead, ask, "Will that new job across town help me fulfill my Divine plan?" If you receive a yes, then ask, " Is a move part of my Divine plan?"

The third part is to request how you receive the answer. You could say, "I would like a simply yes or no." Then once you ask the question, try to see the two words, yes and no, in your mind at the same time, next to each other. Which of the two is easier to see? Which stands out? Which is pulsing or doing something to get your attention? Is one just not appearing no matter how much you try to see it? The one standing out or clearly getting your attention is the intuitive answer to your question. It's really that simple.

Let's look at a few more techniques I use and teach for calling on intuition from my mental field. Often, questions are not so black and white, and can't be answered by a simple yes or no. You may desire more information. So, I often ask to see two or up to three paths in my mind. I have each path represent a possible answer, and then I allow myself to walk along the path in my mind and notice what I see, how I feel and if any Intuitive Footprints trigger. So taking the example above, "Should I take that new job across town?" I would label one path "Yes" and one path "No."

Now that I have my questions and know how I want to receive the information, I can start. I Relax, Step Back repeat the question in my mind and state I will see two paths, the one on the right represents yes and the other path represents no. As I allow myself to imagine walking down the first path, I notice what's there. What's the road I'm walking on like? Is it dirt, graveled, or paved? What's the scenery like? Are there trees or plants; if so, how plentiful? How do I feel on this path? Are any Intuitive Footprints signaling me while on this path? After a few moments, I just move myself to the second path and repeat the same walk, observing the same things as I did on the first path.

If the path on the left is well paved with large trees, my Intuitive Footprint for gratitude was triggered, and there's lots of grass, and the right path has a gravel road, a few small trees, and mostly dirt, it's clear to me that

"No" is the answer. I don't simply have a yes or no answer, but a sense that if I did take the job across town, it would be a bumpy road with a few small rewards sparsely spread out, represented by the gravel road and sparse amount of greenery. Also, it's clear that I will be grateful that I did not take the job over time.

You can receive intuitive insight on anything; it's only limited by your willingness to try it and your imagination.

Let's say you want to sell your house. Before starting, get your questions and how you want to see the answer. It is necessary sometimes to have an intention set in your mind if you want to create a specific outcome. My intention is to find the best buyer for my home, who will offer a good acceptable price, and who will be happy in their choice. Another question is "When is the best time to put my house on the market to have the best possible offer from a buyer who will be pleased with the purchase?" Finally, I state how I want to receive the information; I want it clearly on a large wall calendar.

Step one: Relax, Step Back. Step two: Ask the questions. Step Three: State how you want to receive the information. Now just allow yourself to see a calendar in your mind. Use your imagination, if necessary, to make it appear. Once you see a wall calendar, you may see the month clearly written on top and the date circled as to the actual day. Or you possibly may see pages being torn off the calendar one at a time. Count the pages. Each page represents a month, so if three pages are torn and you're asking in December, the best time to go on the market for you is March. When it stops tearing pages, it may have a date circled, or just show a number, that would be the date.

While already in this state of intuitive receptivity, quickly ask to see the best possible price to expect from the buyer coming on the date showing on the calendar. State to see it like a bar chart, with the numbers clearly marked on the Y axis so it's easy to see the price where the bar reaches.

For the price, you may see just what you asked to see. A clear bar chart that has the range of prices in your area, with a bar colored in up to a certain number, representing the best price you could get for your home. But be careful, this can be tricky. Yes the best price you can receive is not necessarily the price you'll receive. So wording the questions exactly for what you desire is paramount.

Perfecting the questions often takes more work than the entire intuitive technique will take.

The take away here is that once you start receiving intuition, you can continue to ask, you don't have to stop and start over again with each question. Once in that state, the information will flow. If you feel you're getting too wrapped up in forming your questions and concerns, write it all out and then reenter the intuitive mental state.

There's no limit to the information available to you from this field. There are two problems you come across in this method of calling on intuition. The most common is difficulty distinguishing what you want the answer to be from the answer your intuition is sending you. However, there's a way around this bump in the road. Simply ask a friend to do the technique for you. But don't tell the friend what your question is; just ask them which path looks better, A or B. In your mind, you label the paths just like you did for yourself. Instead of saying right or left you say "A or B" or "H or Q" or "purple or green." It doesn't matter what the choices you give your friend to pick from. Just as long as the choices are lined up in your mind as to what they represent. Or ask your friend to see a bar chart and tell you how high on the axes does the chart climb. You set the questions and how you want your friend to see the answers without letting your friend know your question because you don't want your friend's good intention to interfere with the intuitive answer.

Your friend will have had to learn at least the Relax, Step Back technique first, but what a great resource you each will be for the other. My close friend Chris and I call each other often and simply say, "A" or "B."

The other problem students have with this technique is relying on their imagination. They feel it's just their imagination and not really an intuitive answer. Others have written, "If you can imagine it, you can achieve it." Our imagination is completely necessary in order for intuition to flow freely. As you come to trust the intuition you're receiving on demand, the less concern you'll have about using your imagination. Just jump in with both feet and try it.

Wording your questions carefully and requesting how you wish to receive your answers from your "inner-net" of intuition is one of the most effective tools you can acquire. The mental field is one of the most quickest and accurate ways to retrieve your intuitive information. So much so, it's hard to really believe it at first, creating unnecessary doubt. Most people doubt the validity of something if it's too easy. A wise person sees this as a blessing. Just as you can tap into the mental field surrounding your body, you can also tap into the aura field for intuitive information.

Chapter 8

Seeing Auras

Training yourself to see auras is actually misleading. Seeing the energy and colors around us is a natural ability we all had as children. Some people carry it into adulthood. But without training and openness about the energy, most of us just shut down this ability to see auras. Children, usual under the age of five, can see the auras. Notice how infants frequently look above and around a person, not directly at their face. It's where the colors of the aura are largest around a person.

Once you start seeing the aura, the next question is how this can be useful in my life other than as entertainment. Sure, it's cool and interesting, but really how does it serve me? What intuitive information could be gained to make it worth doing?

The aura is like a mood ring from the 1970s. The color change based on a person's mood. However, the fundamental colors, those that are always present coming in from the mental field, are the core principles held by the person, whose aura you're gazing at. Seeing the aura allows you to understand immediately what a person holds as their core principles and what mood they are in at any moment.

Suppose a woman is about to get married but can't choose between two good friends as to which one should be the maid of honor Her oldest and dearest friend has green coming into her aura, but the green is murky and dull. While her more recent friend from work has a light bright vibrant yellow. The colors all have meanings, both positive and negative. (See Appendix F) The murky dull green implies the old friend is envious, green with envy. The vibrant yellow indicates the newer friend is developing her spiritual qualities. This simple gaze of looking at the aura can change a lot of unhappy wedding day scenarios.

You can practice seeing auras anywhere at any time and nobody will ever know. The world is loaded with volunteers. Every plant, animal and person you see is waiting for you to practice seeing their auras. As with all techniques, when you're ready, tell yourself, "Relax, step-back." Now you're in the relaxed state necessary to tap into the whole consciousness and are ready to point your laser focus to the question or concern at hand.

Ask yourself, while in this state, "I wonder what this person's aura looks like?" Be in a curious state, relaxed, childlike. Nobody will know if you don't see anything because nobody knows your looking. Just relax, be playful, and it will appear to you. While in the relaxed, step back mental state, there's nothing to be achieved; it's a state of witnessing. So simply allow yourself the time and freedom to witness auras. It's great to just gaze at your own hand and ask, "I wonder what my aura looks like?"

To help myself, when I first was training, I would often imagine what that person's aura looked like, even when I did not see anything. I simply kept imagining until one day, I started seeing.

It is helpful to have a soft gaze, and don't look directly at a person, instead have your gaze looking around the etheric field of a person. Auras will begin to appear over time, for some people it comes almost immediately. For other it takes more time to get back to that childlike gaze necessary to see. Although children see auras, to them it's natural. The ability unfortunately goes dormant from lack of use or acknowledgment. We all know that skills we use stay with us as we grow; others just go dormant. The wonderful thing is there's nothing to learn; simply Relax, Step Back and allow yourself to see.

Often, the aura will not appear in all its full colors, but start more simply. Usually a person will see the etheric energy field around the other person, which looks like a shadow outline. Relax into seeing what's just beyond the etheric, in the astral body, and the aura will appear. Give yourself permission to have fun with it. As you begin to see the energy fields, even if there's no color, notice the brightness and width. The more you practice, and hold the intention of seeing auras, the sooner you will.

Take notice when it's easy to see auras and when it's not. Is it when your energy is on the upswing that you see better? Do you see auras indoors better than in the natural light? Notice these things; just as with all skills in life, we're better at doing them in some places and times than others.

During a job interview, you might see that your prospective employer's aura is driven by strength and vitality, and he balances materialism with warmth and affection. These are usually indicated by a vibrant red. Or, the prospective employer might be greedy with a possible tendency toward cruelty displayed in the dark dull red in the aura. The beneficial information available by seeing and properly interpreting auras is endless.

I was with my oldest child, who was just a teenager at the time. He heard me speaking about energy and proceeded to explain how he sees and plays with the energy field himself. He was surprised to learn that I didn't see it at that time. It was such a natural state to him; he thought everyone saw energy fields, colors, and symbols. Interestingly, it took a young person to bring the ability, the awareness of seeing auras, back to me. Within an hour, I was exploring everything around me and just playing like a child in a sandbox. He encouraged me to start looking at the energy around plants and animals. It was so much fun experimenting with the aura energy moving from our hands to a plant on the table. We watched how far we could move our fingers from the plant before the energy link would break and the energy would just move back into our hands and the plant.

Auras are excellent for diagnosing medical concerns in animals and children who are too young to speak, which will be covered in the chapter on medical intuition. Seeing auras is not a learned skill; it's just a reawakening of a dormant skill. The next chapter on psychometry is about feeling the energy on an object, but interestingly enough, inanimate objects have auras also. So while learning to read the energy you feel, you can practice your ability to see auras.

Chapter 9

Psychometry

Psychometry is reading the energy from an inanimate object. Our energy is left everywhere, we are dropping it on everything we pass and everything we touch. The longer an item is in our personal possession the stronger the energy patterns are left on that item. Psychometry is simply reading the energy from these items to provide insight on a person who came into contact with the item. The more you use any of these techniques to assist you with gathering information, the easier it becomes.

I'm sure you've used psychometry and just don't realize you have. Have you ever picked up an item at a yard sale, and felt instantly connected to it? As if there was something about this piece, you just could not explain, but you had to have it? So you find yourself with this fifty cent vase, you don't need. Most likely, that vase was used often to hold flowers and it was well appreciated by its owner. The appreciation the originally owner had for the vase when using it, is imprinted on the vase as an energy. You pick up the vase, and feel a sense of appreciation or even love.

The opposite is also often true. You may find the perfect piece of used furniture, great price, excellent condition, right size, you think you need, but for some reason it just doesn't speak to you, or it just doesn't feel right. You're reading the energy on that object and are not even aware you are.

We pick up information on new items also, just not as frequently. New items have some imprint left from the factory, to the trucker, to the stock person, and every customer who picked it up or felt it before you. That's why we don't usually have strong emotional reactions to newer items that we do when we touch used items.

I've found, over the years, that instructors have placed restrictions on all of these exercises in one form or another. Some restrictions I've heard include the item you read can only have been owned by one person. Nonsense, just set your intention the information to be received from the object be only related to the person in question. There's no object that's off limits and there's no proper way to hold the object; it's all very personal. I will explain the basic way to learn psychometry. As you experiment with this technique, you'll find ways that it serves you best.

Like all exercises, first Relax, Step Back. Set your intention. For example, "I intend to find the best babysitter for my children." Next, hold the object of the person you want to receive information about. Using our babysitter example, when the prospective sitter leaves your house, sit in the chair she sat in. Yes, you can get information from your bottom as easily as you can your hands, feet, or anything. While sitting in the chair, ask your question, "Is the woman who sat in the chair a good, safe, mindful sitter who will watch after my children lovingly?" Now notice the Intuitive Footprints that start to appear. Did you get a signal that this person has anger issues, or did your joyful Intuitive Footprint trigger? Do you feel like you just have to get out of the chair, or do you want to curl up in the chair because it's so welcoming?

With psychometry, you're identifying information in two ways. First, you're noticing the subtle energy by identifying the Intuitive Footprint. The

Intuitive Footprint provides the not-so-obvious information. Second, you're noticing how the object makes you feel. How do you relate to the feeling? If the feeling brings back to you the same feelings you had as a child being bullied, then you know the person related to the object may be a bully or was bullied. Ask yourself, "Was this person bullied?" Ask to see the answer in a Yes or No form, just as in the "Trusting Your Mind" chapter. The best way to call forth intuition is to not limit it to any one method at any time. Intertwining these methods will give your intuition many roads to communicate with you on demand. You'll be able to apply many of those techniques at the same time, eventually finding the way that you work best with your own intuition.

My favorite way to use psychometry is to find lost items. You misplaced your keys, you know they are in your house, but don't know where. Take a piece of paper and quickly draw the rooms in your home. You may even add large pieces of furniture, so to have a better idea of where to look upon completing the exercise. Once you finish drawing the rooms, place the paper on a table in front of you and follow these steps:

Relax, Step Back. Set your intention, "It's my intention to find my keys in a few minutes." Visualize your keys; see your keys clearly in your mind. The next step is to scan the maps you just drew gently with your fingertips. Allow your hand to glide over the pages in an even motion, till you scanned all the paper. Notice the room where the energy feels different than the rest of the paper. Once you distinguish the room, start scanning the room on the paper to locate the exact place in the room where you'll find your keys. Again you're feeling for energy that's different than that felt on the rest of the page.

A few years back, my dog Sheba ran away. She was just adopted by a young couple and was at her new home. Sheba appeared to fit right in with the other dog and cat, and the new owners fell in love with her instantly. We were so blessed to know Sheba would be welcomed into a new home and not forced to remain locked in a small room away from my grandson. Well, the joy disappeared when I received a call that Sheba bolted for the door and ran away. Unbeknownst to us, this is common when a dog is taken from one home to another. The energy is different, and they're just looking for the familiar energy of their family. After all, we were part of her pack.

The whole night, my husband and oldest son drove the neighborhood of her new family, hoping to find her. The next morning, I pulled out a street map of the neighborhood. While my husband drove, I followed the instructions above. Relaxed, and stepped back. Set my intention that the map will guide me to Sheba. I began sweeping the map with my fingers. After a couple of pages, I noticed a rough spot on the map; it felt different than all the other spots. My husband drove directly to the area I was pointing to and proceeded driving up and down the few streets to no avail. I again scanned the map and my fingers were stuck like glue, they would not come off the area we were currently searching. I knew without a doubt, Sheba was there; we just didn't see her.

With tears flowing down my face, I told my husband to get signs and post them around the area. As we pulled out, we received a phone call from the new adopting family. They told us the dog catcher found Sheba the previous night and she was being brought back to them shortly. We discovered the dog catcher was located exactly where my fingers were on the map. We had passed his office several times.

My emotional upset of not finding Sheba, even though my fingers where stuck on the map, prevented me from asking my higher self, my mental field for more details. Emotions play a strong role and can prevent you from observing with laser focus attention. I'm sure my Intuitive Footprint triggered every time we passed the police station, but I was not laser focused, my emotions were distracting my attention.

Psychometry can be used for many useful common things in life. You're moving to a new city and aren't sure what neighborhood would best suit your family needs. You Relax, Step Back and ask, "What neighborhood will best serve my needs and those of my family?" Scan that city's maps with your fingertips till your fingers feel something different than the way they felt on the rest of the map. Often, it will feel like something sticky or a very slight resistance.

While living in your new perfect neighborhood, your tooth starts to hurt. Pull out the phone book, Relax, Step Back; ask, "What dentist will best serve my needs as far as price and excellent care?" Now scan the phone book using the same technique. There are no limits with this technique. Scan for a restaurant. Relax, Step Back and ask, "What restaurant makes chicken parmesan the way I like?" In my hometown of South Philly there are so many excellent Italian restaurants that it could take a year of eating out and only ordering chicken parmesan to find the perfect one. It's a lot faster and satisfying to scan the phone book under Italian restaurants.

Psychometry is using the energy on an object to provide you information. That information can be about a specific person, such as a babysitter, or it can be something for your personal use, like finding a good place to eat.

Sometimes you can't be where the object or person for whom you need information is. Sometimes, they're across the country or on the other side of the world. That's when you use remote viewing.

Chapter 10

Remote Viewing

Russell Targ, physicist and cofounder of the Stanford Research Institute, describes remote viewing in his book *"Limitless Mind"* as, "the awareness of the individual is not separate from (or "contiguous with") a specific target at a distant location" (Targ, 2010, p. 9). In other words, it "can be described as the result of an apparent zero separation between the viewer and the target." The only thing more difficult to understand than tapping into intuition is understanding a physicist. But physicists come the closest to understanding how time and space don't exist in the world of intuition.

The Nobel Prize in Physics was awarded to Drs. Haroche and Wineland for proving that electrons can be in two places at the same time. Both these seemingly bizarre facts about physics, zero-separation and one electron in two different places at the same time, lend a great deal of credence to the process of remote viewing. During a remote viewing, the viewer knows they are in a chair where they started the exercise, but are just as sure they are seeing somewhere else or sometime else. A viewer can go back in time or forward into the future. This almost sounds like science fiction, but it's not.

Remote viewing is one of the most accurate ways to tap into the universal energy field where all information exists simultaneously. In fact, it gives you much more than a hunch, it will draw you a complete picture, limited only by your concern that it's your imagination. The process requires a strong intention set in the mental field of our energy, and then simultaneously expanding and contracting different energy fields to explore based on the intention. Remote viewing is NOT astral projection. Astral projection is allowing our astral energy field, or electromagnetic field, to project forward, leaving the physical body while seeking the information. This is not safe, and I strongly discourage it, because it leaves the body empty and open to dangers. Remote viewing is an advanced technique. I prefer my students to have several months tapping into their intuition before they attempt this method.

All the exercises described require an interest in the experiment and an intention being set. The same applies to remote viewing; intention and interest are key. Have your question clear in your mind. What information are you seeking? Just as with all the others, you start off giving yourself the suggestion to Relax, Step Back. Set your intention. "I intend to gather information on ...(state your intention)." You can ask additional questions as answers flow into your mind.

At this point, you allow your energy fields to expand and contract simultaneously.

Now, for a quick review of all three energy fields: etheric, astral, and mental, note they are intertwine. You cannot affect one without the others being affected in a nanosecond. So as you expand from the mental field into the universal source of all energy, you pull your astral and etheric fields inward toward your body. Allow the energy to expand upward gradually moving out as it moves up. This holds a strong connection to your physical body. Use your imagination at first. In a short period of time, you'll start to physically feel this pulling and pushing. It is comfortable and natural. If you could see the energy, it appears as if you're inside a protected eggshell where the energy moves upward into infinity.

An analogy to assist in understanding the concept is to think of a balloon. When a balloon is being inflated, the air inside pushes outwards on the rubber of the balloon, expanding its size dramatically. At the same time the rubber of the balloon is expanding, it is also contracting inward on the air being forced into it, holding the balloon shape. Imagine you're expanding and contracting simultaneously like a balloon being inflated.

If at any time, it doesn't feel comfortable and natural, stop for a while before trying again.

If you feel entering a peaceful mode, you're doing it right. Now, imagine this perfectly peaceful silence merging with you, enveloping you. Merge with it, and notice you're holding your own space and integrity while still completely engulfed by this perfect peaceful silence. In this place, you'll being to remote view. The information will come as pictures, sounds, smells, symbols, and countless other ways. Eventually, this peaceful silence will start to pull away, indicting all the information you need has been provided. At that time, pull your energies inward, give thanks, and immediately write down or speak into a recorder everything you felt or experienced.

It's best to document your impressions immediately. The process you experienced is similar to dreaming; you've crossed the opaque vale to the dimension where all things and all times exist simultaneously. Once back on this side of the vale, information begins to slip away. You may think you'll remember, but just like the full bladder calling you out of bed has you forgetting that awesome dream, so will life on this side have you forget the awesome insights. Record them immediately.

This process can be used to retrieve precognitive intuitive information, future data. I use this technique before every long-distance trip I take. Within a minute or less I know if I will go and arrive home safely. Several years ago, I went to Lebanon with my parents. Not really the safest place in the world, but at the time, there had not been anything disturbing for a few years. So, I took just a minute, set my intention, and had my question. "Will this trip to Lebanon be safe for my parents and me?" I saw myself and my parents enter a plane, followed by exiting it, followed by entering again and finally exiting it again. There was no emotional upset present, it felt normal and relaxed, and all three of us were together in all four images. I clearly received a message we would all leave and arrive together safely in Lebanon and returning home.

There are endless possibilities for remote viewing. It's the most versatile form of tapping into the inner-net of intuition on demand than all the others combined. It's easy to implement other techniques while using this one.

There are so many possibilities. When I first was being professionally trained to master my intuitive abilities, not just exploring on my own, my mentor sent me a photo inside two envelopes. It was my assignment to see what my intuition would tell me about the person in the picture. I Relaxed, Stepped Back, and began to expand and contract with the intention to discover who this person was and what information I was to report. I hit an invisible wall, a wall of strong resistance, which told me this person did not want to be read.

I pulled myself back and did some quick soul searching. I knew my mentor would never ask me to gather intuitive information on someone who did not give permission to be a part of this exercise. So I regrouped and decided to push beyond this invisible wall of resistance. I gathered the information requested of me such as the person's sex, age, occupation, personality traits, personal concerns, desires, etc. Upon gathering the intuitive information I needed, I turned the information over to my mentor and waited to hear the response. The woman who's picture was in the two envelopes, called me personally after reviewing the information.

She was amazed I could gather so much information about her. She expressed that she had intentionally put this wall of resistance up, and not even professional psychics had been able to get information due to this wall. I'm not telling you this to brag. I knew I had the years of practice, which equipped me to pass this wall. My mentor understood this woman had agreed to this test. She knew I would not invade the privacy of her will. I'm telling you so you understand the importance of honoring such resistance. Don't press forward. This woman agreed because she knew I could not break past her will to remain private. We are never to impose our will on another. If such a wall or resistance appears, pull back. Our intuition is stating the other person does not wish to share information at this time.

There have been times in my practice when someone would insist that I move into areas or do something else to assist them, even though there was another who didn't wish this involvement. I always turned down the work. It's not my place to ever impose my will or another's will on someone else, even if I believe it to be a good cause. God's greatest proof of his love for us is our free will. He doesn't impose his will on us, even though he knows better. Why should we assume to know better? Point of the story, an invisible block or push back is a universal footprint that's saying, "Don't go forward; it's against this person's will."

Remember, universal footprints are those Intuitive Footprints that are exactly the same for everyone. We experience most every Intuitive Footprint differently, but "Something's Wrong" and "Push Back" are a couple of the universal footprints that feel exactly the same for everyone.

The following story is why I don't use astral projection anymore and will only practice remote viewing. For years, I practiced using astral projection, so by the time of this incident, I was already receiving useful information regularly.

For a few years, I worked with a unique group of individuals from the Edgar Cayce's Association of Research and Enlightenment called the Battered Boundaries. Our group was committed to helping people who were suffering from disturbing, intrusive, or other unwanted psychic experience.

Astral projection was an indispensable tool for gathering information and assisting those in trouble. From my comfortable favorite chair, I would travel to where the person was and start checking the area for what was creating the issue causing the client to suffer. I found this technique one of the most useful and fastest ways to gather accurate information, till one day...

On that morning, while driving to work, a thought came to mind that I needed to find out more about Malachi Martin. I knew Malachi Martin was a Roman Catholic priest who did exorcisms, and I had previously read one of his books. This thought was so loud and out of place, I knew immediately my intuition was trying to give me a message. Often this happens when the message is urgent. So the question remained, "Why am I being compelled suddenly to need to learn more about this priest?"

My job at the time, afforded me the ability to listen to anything I wished while working. So I quickly pulled up some interviews on YouTube featuring Malachi Martin. As I moved through my day, I was very captivated on what this amazing man was sharing. Then I heard Father Martin say, "Never, ever, mind travel." Mind travel and astral projection are used interchangeably. He explained in detail how dangerous this is spiritually and how it opens you to demonic possession.

Well, I just knew Father Martin was wrong. I started arguing, out loud with an interview that was over 30 years old. Thank goodness I had a private office. I argued, clearly from my personal experience, I had proof of dozens of people I helped using this technique. I continued my argument that with proper preparation and prayer, I was safe and you (Malachi) are obviously wrong! I decided this priest may know a whole lot, but nobody's perfect, so I just continued to listen and see what else he had to say because I was sure some of it would be useful for me.

Not 10 minutes after hearing his outrageous statement to never use astral projection, my cell phone rang. It was a client who I had helped in the past from Texas. A year prior, she had been experiencing unexplained extreme psychic experiences in her antique shop. She said she could actually see large groups of ghosts, very sad lost souls, marching through her store, along with other experiences. I used astral projection to see what was causing this attraction of spirits to her store.

In one trip, I was able to identify the object and provide her with a complete explanation why this object was attracting these lost souls. I discussed the proper way to handle the item and she followed my advice. She did not call again except once to say everything was great and she really appreciated my help. Not bad. Take that Malachi!

Wait a minute? Why was it on this day that I felt this sudden urge to learn more about Malachi Martin? This is what most people call a coincidence; I call it intuition. My higher self was warning me. Sure enough, my old client was experiencing something else in her shop and asked if I could do "that thing" I did before for her. Instead of saying yes, I found myself second guessing and stated I would do what I could and get back to her.

When I was home and ready to assist this client, it wasn't easy for me to fight the urge to astral project to her location. I relied heavily on and enjoyed this technique I used. This time, I was struggling to keep my spirit in my body. Normally, it would just take off and go. It took tremendous effort, but I stayed put and just asked from my chair what was occurring in Texas at the location of the antique store, using remote viewing method instead. Never leaving my body, being fully present, while expanding outward. I felt this tremendous angry push of energy come toward me. It clearly meant to cause me harm. I would have been extremely vulnerable if I had been astral projecting and not solidly in my body.

After regrouping and remaining calm, I said my prayers and went back into position to safely remote view for answers. The intuitive information was clear: the woman in Texas was under partial possession by the devil and so was her store. She needed help immediately. We spoke shortly after I had all my information and I was glad to hear she was in full agreement. She said she had recently been seeing a priest who was trying to get her the proper help from his bishop for an exorcism. She had not share the information with me, because she was hoping I would just be able to make it all go away. In the Catholic Church, exorcisms cannot be performed without express permission of the bishop.

Why am I telling you this story? Well, from that day on, I never astral traveled again. The thought to listen to Malika Martin out of the blue was an intuitive blessing sent from above to keep me safe. Out of the dozens of Malika Martin interviews online, I just happened to listen to the one that warn never to mind travel/astral project. I heeded that warning; I wouldn't have been able to completely protect myself from the evil charging toward me. Out of my body, I was extremely vulnerable to evil taking over of my spirit.

During astral travel, the astral energy field leaves the physical body. The astral field is the curious field, the one that likes to explore. It's the energy field that often has you thinking of someone just before that person calls. It's neither your soul nor your spirit; it's one of your energy bodies discussed in Chapter 4. When one of these three major fields is affected, the other two are also affected in a nanosecond. So the physical discomfort, even pain, being thrown at the astral body will be felt by the physical body and the mental body.

The mental body is where one's spirit communes with its highest self, God. So, if the astral body is suddenly attacked, it will affect the spirit, given that it dwells in the mental field. Possession cannot occur without one's consent, but the evil can hurt a spirit in other ways. It can inflict physical pain to levels that cause a person to accept possession, believing it will make the pain stop. It can cause confusing thoughts, leading to mental illness. The purpose of this book it to teach you how to safely access your inner-net of intuitive knowledge; for this reason, I strongly recommend never using astral travel.

This story reinforces why I teach remote viewing instead of astral projection. Some will go ahead and explore with astral projection, which is their free will. Others will think twice and decide on the other techniques in this book, which are safe if done following all the instructions. I do believe if you're properly prepared, you'll be protected as I was. Because I did the necessary spiritual and energy work, I was attuned to the warning.

Remote viewing is a powerful tool to gathering massive amounts of information quickly. Like all the other exercises, you start with Relax, Step Back, set your intention and questions, and proceed. The information from this area will often come as symbols and signs, which require additional understanding and interpreting on your part. The best advice is use the understanding you feel best fits a particular symbol or sign, not what a book tells you it means. This information is coming for you specifically; the signs or symbols are personal to you. Out of all the techniques I teach, this is truly one of my favorite. When performed correctly, it's as if you had a personal coaching session with God.

Not all intuitive messages are for us; some are to help those who are ill. This is Medical Intuition and it's a very sacred process.

Chapter 11

Medical Intuition

We proceed first with common sense. Medical intuition is never to replace the advice of a medical physician. It can and will provide valuable information. But I don't suggest you walk into your doctor's office and declare your child need his gallbladder surgically removed because you saw black spots around that area of his aura. You may have picked up an energy block, or disturbance of the gallbladder, but leave the diagnosing to the doctor. Instead, use the information to send healing energy to your child and continue to monitor the area. Use common sense and always follow the advice of a medical doctor. In Chapter 12, we will discuss healing.

So with this disclaimer aside, and trusting the reader has common sense, let's learn how to use medical intuition and why it can be helpful. As all the other exercises, the first thing is the Relax, Step Back technique. Once in this relaxed state, bring your laser- sharp attention to the person or animal you wish to scan for possible energy disturbances. There are two excellent techniques for scanning a body for disturbances. But first, let's define what is meant by disturbance.

An energy disturbance is simply a difference in the way the energy feels to the rest of the body. It's not a medical diagnosis, it's not an indication of illness, and it's not an indication of pending death. It's simply sensing or seeing that something is not flowing the way it usually does, and, therefore, is different. Just like psychometry, you're feeling for something that feels different from the rest of that body. The first techniques requires you to scan a person's field with your hands. The second techniques requires you to simply ask their etheric field to show you the areas of disturbance.

Please remember when scanning anyone that the person is trusting you to enter into their personal space, so be caring and loving. Come from a mental intention of "wanting to be of service." The healings chapter will go into greater detail as to why being in a loving state of service is important for you as well as the person you're scanning.

Next thing to remember is that energy is always moving. When you approach a person to scan, do so in a gentle manner. Allow your hands to dive in fingertips first to just above the etheric field. Imagine you have a bowl of water in front of you and the water represents the energy surrounding a body. If you bring your hands palms first into the water, you'll splash it everywhere, and it will take time for the water to become still again. However, if you place your hands gently into the water, fingertips first, moving unrushed and gracefully the water will only be disturbed for a moment. The same with that body's energy.

By now, you should know to start with Relax, Step Back, state your intention so your mental field is working with you. "It is my intent to be of service and to discover where there are any energy disturbances." Next, create an energy ball between your hands, and expand the ball large enough so that you can encapsulate the person to be scanned and their body is inside the energy ball between your hands. As you walk toward the person with the energy ball, lead with your fingertips and move gently and gracefully until your hands are around their head. One palm faces the person's forehead while the other palm, the back of the head.

The technique for scanning is simple. The key to successfully scanning is having your laser-sharp attention focused on your palms to sense the energy. While holding one hand steady, slowly move the energy ball with the second hand in a circular motion while moving down one side of the body. Do not try to scan the entire front or back of the person at once. That would require you stepping too closely to their personal space, which, besides being rude, could cause a temporary disturbance. Once you have scanned the half closest to you, move to the other side, form a new energy ball and scan the second half. You'll need to scan the person four times to cover the entire body. The four scans will cover the right side front, left side front, right side rear, and left side rear.

During the process of scanning, stay laser focused on what you're feeling. Where are you feeling it? And what does it feel like? Make mental notes as to what you feel and where you feel it. What does the disturbance feel like? What am I distinguishing different in this area than the other areas? What makes it different? Does it have a color? Temperature? Texture?

Upon the completion of the last scan, disperse the energy that has collected on your hands into the floor or wall. You do this by placing your hands on the floor or wall exhaling a long steady breath and inviting all the energy that's not yours to leave your body. Then discuss with the person what you felt, but not your interpretation of what you felt. For example, let's say you felt a pulling of energy at the eyes. Your interpretation may be the person has the beginning stages of cataracts. Avoid any and all interpretation; just focus on the disturbance. You're not a physician, so interpreting the data is dangerous. Most likely, the person is simply wearing contacts, and now you have them frightened out of their wits because you diagnosed by interpreting.

The usefulness of this method is in the healing that can be provided by the person providing the scanning.

You're feeling for energies that are different from most of the body. A place that feels cooler or warmer, an area that produces resistance or feels sticky, are changes in the energy field to note.

It's best to find some good friends willing to allow you to practice this technique on them. The more you practice, the more quickly you'll be able to scan a body for disturbances. As in all the other exercises, your skill will increase exponentially. Eventually, you'll be able to sense the energy quickly and react to it appropriately. The fact that you practice sensing your own energy will have already sensitized your hands to disturbances.

This first method of medical intuition through scanning is very personal. It requires being close and actively feeling for the disturbance. However, the second method is much easier, and I've found that it provides much more details. The second method I call "Asking."

In the Asking Method of medical intuition, the first step is of course to Relax, Step Back. Once in that relaxed state, I state my intention silently to myself: "I intend to be of service and to discover where there are any energy disturbances on (name the person)." Next, I simply ask the person's etheric field to step forward and show me where there are disturbances. At first you may need to image this shadow figure stepping alongside or in front of the person about whom you're asking information. You can't do it if you can't imagine it first. Be childlike and image the etheric shadow figure is standing clearly in your mind.

The next step is to mentally ask the figure to point to or demonstrate where there are disturbances you can possible help with by sending healing. The figure may point to its right knee, indicating there's a disturbance, or to ears, or even its teeth. Don't assume when a figure points to the heart there are problems with the heart muscle. It could be indicating a broken heart or heartburn. None of the interpretations matter because our intent is not to diagnosis but to send healing to where the figure says disturbances are located. Once all the information is presented, thank the etheric field for providing the information and ask it to return to its proper place.

This method of asking the etheric field has helped me personally care for one of my aging dogs. While away at an all-day conference, I sensed my oldest dog, Duke, was having difficulty. So I simply did the Relax, Step Back, and set my intention, which was to understand what was happening with Duke and help if I could. Next, I asked his etheric field to show me what was going on. I saw the shadow of his etheric field limping and struggling more than usually to get up from a sitting position. All around his hips was a chalky looking substance. I began the process of sending healing.

When I arrived home, Duke was jumping like a puppy, running all around. He greeted me and would not leave me alone the rest of the day, as if he were saying, "I know what you did, and thanks." Animals don't tell us what's wrong with them; we can only guess by the way they look at us. Neither can young children. That's why medical intuition can bring them early healing.

There are a few very important things to remember when scanning anyone. First, the person is trusting you to enter into their personal space, so be caring and loving. Come from a mental state of service. Second, our energies begin to blend together as soon as we're within a few feet, sometimes sooner. If you're sending loving thoughts of service, no negative emotions or illnesses can trace back into your field and cause you illness. However, if you're trying to scan from a place of ego, from a place of look at me and what I can do, you're more open to attracting disturbances into your field from the person you're scanning. This is an important warning that will be covered more thoroughly in the healing chapter.

Chapter 12

Healings

There's no point in using medical intuition if you're not going to use the intuitive information you receive to assist the person. It is like asking a friend for advice. There's no point if you're not going to use it. So let's learn how to heal, so you use the medical intuition input being sent to you.

Healing is done from a loving state of service. The mechanics are relatively simply. The energy of Universal Source comes into the healer through the crown chakra down to the heart chakra. From the heart chakra, the healer takes Universal Source energy and directs it down their arms, into their hands, and into the energy field of the person they wish to serve. This technique requires the ability to sense the subtle energy in your hands, so you don't overcharge them with energy.

Healers are givers, using their time for a higher purpose. It is very selfless. There are many forms of healing, prayer being the most powerful. As a young teenager, I was fortunate to have parents with a home library of books that ranged from encyclopedias for children to Shakespeare. On the shelves, when just browsing out of boredom, I came across one of Francis Macnutt's books on healing. It was written when he was still a Catholic priest and he spoke clearly on the power of healing energy to move through a willing healer into the person in need. It was so simple and it made sense. I've since read almost all his books. I would recommend his work to anyone interested in being a healer. He has workshops with his wife in Florida and there's plenty of information available online.

Healing prayers can be done in similar ways. The method I use begins with a prayer. Ask to be a clear channel of God's blessings so His Will may be done through you and in service to the person, animal, or situation. When working on a person, gently place your hands on their shoulders and allow the energy, which is filling you and accumulating in your heart chakra, to flow into their shoulders. During this process, you're conscious of your station, which is serving as a conduit between grace and the person. Usually, after several minutes, depending on the amount of physical, mental, or spiritual healing needed, you'll have an Intuitive Footprint that lets you know it's time to remove your hands.

As with most Intuitive Footprints, it will be specific to you. I've found most people experience this Intuitive Footprint as a sensation somewhere in their hands. Often it will feel like the receiver's energy pushes your hands back either abruptly or very subtly. Once you remove your hands, say a quick prayer of thanks. That's it. Nice and simple.

When working with an animal, if possible, lay your hands on the animal. We don't necessarily have to touch a person or animal for energy to flow freely. But there's no doubt in the power of healing that comes from touch. You'll do the same steps as with a person. Start with a prayer, ask to be a clear channel, allow the energy to flow through you from above, wait for the Intuitive Footprint that says to stop, remove your hands, and close with a prayer of thanks.

In healing an emotional problem, the technique is the same, except you cannot put hands on that situation per se. Instead, you can face your palms outward in front of you and send the healing to the situation. Hold in your mind the intention of healing being sent to the particular situation. You hold this position again till your Intuitive Footprint says it's time to stop. An example would be two coworkers who are bickering and causing an uncomfortable work environment for everyone else. Go to the restroom, Relax, Step Back, state your intention to be a conduit of God's grace so this situation can be healed, stretch your arms outward in front of you with your palms facing out, and hold till you feel your Intuitive Footprint stop.

Rarely do you ever direct the energy; it's your job to just be the conduit. However, there are times when your intuition will demand you do something more with the Divine energy. Earlier, I mentioned how I asked my dog Duke's etheric field to show me what was bothering him. The field showed me chalk on his hips. The fact the etheric field did not stop at the inability to stand up easily, but actually showed me an image of chalk, let me know that when I sent the energy forward (remember I was not home at the time), I was to direct it to erase the chalk. So I used my imagination to direct the energy and imagined there was an eraser in my hand, simply erasing the chalk.

Love is the most powerful energy known. It transmutes all other energies to its vibration. You're protected from absorbing negative energies or that person's illness because you're sending out love. Jesus, who many see as pure love, stated, "I have come into the world as light, so that whoever believes in me may not remain in darkness" (John 12:46 ESV). Where there's love, there's light. Where there's light, there can be no darkness. So love transmutes the darkness, be it illness or disagreements or anything in need of healing. As you send pure love, it's transmuting the darkness; it cannot move toward you.

I often think of Walt Disney's classic fairy characters. They were always good and were of service to someone. Whenever one of these fairies flew, they would leave tiny light particles fluttering behind them. It's as if Walt Disney understood pure love is light. His little fairies where representations of pure love.

The more you work with people, the more you begin to see we are all connected in some way. So, the healing of one is actually healing many. When healing takes place, it has no time or space limits. Physicists Drs. Haroche and Wineland proved one electron can be in two places at the same time and physicist Russell Targ speaks of zero-separation, where time and places exist simultaneously. These three lend credence to healing through time. Healing goes into a person's past and future simultaneously.

The following was taken from an article called "Wellness Implications of Retroactive Intentional Influence: Exploring an Outrageous Hypothesis." It supports the facts healing occurring through the target's past present and future time simultaneously.

Virtually all medical and psychological treatments and interventions—conventional as well as complementary and alternative—are assumed to act in present time on present, already well-established conditions. An alternative healing pathway is proposed in which healing intentions—in the form of direct mental interactions with biological systems—may act in a "backward," time-displaced manner to influence probabilities of initial occurrence of earlier "seed moments" in the development of illness or health. Because seed moments are more labile, freely variable, and flexible, as well as unusually sensitive to small influences, time-displaced healing pathways may be especially efficacious. This unusual hypothesis is supported by a review of a substantial database of well-controlled laboratory experiments. Theoretical rationales and potential health applications and implications are presented. (Braud, 2000, p. 37)

So you're not just serving a person in the present should you opt to channel love. You're healing the history that contributed to the physical problem or emotional disturbances not only to and in the present but also in the future.

There's only one possible drawback to learning and practicing these techniques with which you're able to call on your intuition anytime. And, that is, it will make you more Empathic.

Chapter 13

Empaths Just Do It a Little Differently

Now, just what is an empath? Empaths are very sensitive people who pick up on emotions around them, often unbeknownst to them, causing the empath not to understand why they are overwhelmed, nervous, and afraid. Many people are empathic and suffer from traits of emotional and even physical pain, simply because they're not aware that what they're feeling is not coming from them. We are all empathic to some degree.

People who are very empathic are often labeled overly sensitive or moody due to their heightened sensitivity. Undiagnosed, empaths pick up energies from all around them, including animals and inanimate objects. Often, they suddenly experience headaches or feel depressed, angry, or sad without rhyme or reason. This can possibly lead to severe depression, extreme shyness, avoidance of public areas, and feelings of anxiousness.

However, once an empath realizes the emotions and physical sensations they feel are not coming *from* them but *to* them, it's more easily controlled and can be used to assist in enhancing their intuition. Basically, anyone experiencing any type of unexplained illness, tiredness, whether an empath or not, can do the following process to determine if the emotion is coming from or to them. Most empaths will own the physical or emotional pain, until they realize it's something they can identify using the Relax, Step Back exercise.

Upon realizing you're overwhelmed or sensing a negative emotion without reason, you need to begin the steps for Relax, Step Back exercise and feel for an Intuitive Footprint on your body. When that occurs, you need to identify that problem and ask from where this is coming from? You learn that it's not your emotions because you felt an Intuitive Footprint matching the emotion overwhelming you. At that point, you start the process of disconnecting from the emotion.

If that Intuitive Footprint is not present, then this emotion is yours. When there's a footprint, it's coming from another; footprints or other people's emotions imprint on your body. Once the Intuitive Footprint, let's say sadness, is identified, it's imperative that you state clearly to yourself, "This is not mine; I don't need to feel it." Usually several deep breaths helps. Miraculously, the emotion will vanish, as will physical pain if handled in the same manner. The difference between an empath and most other people is that the empath doesn't have to go looking for the emotion; the unwelcomed emotion finds the empath.

My favorite example of being overwhelmed, as I became more empathic, was when I visited the Gettysburg battlefield with my husband. Bad move! I advise all empaths to avoid battlefields, especially in communities that keep the history alive. We were walking along the main street and decided to stop into an antique store. While browsing, I was suddenly hit with extreme anger, hatred, and physical heaviness in my chest. Having worked with Relax, Step Back exercise for years, I automatically moved into that position to figure out what was happening. I knew from past experience the Intuitive Footprints my body was experiencing was telling me there was an entire section of Nazi memorabilia at the end of the row I was standing in, and I needed to leave to avoid feeling any more of the pain coming from the inanimate objects.

I could have stood my ground, declared that these were not emotions, and closed myself off from feeling the pain. But I was so exhausted from constantly closing myself from the battlefield pains, I chose instead to leave. The point being, I knew what was causing the problem, instead of thinking I was having chest pains and becoming angry or nasty toward my husband. My husband confirmed my findings and suggested, to my relief, we leave Gettysburg at that point.

I took the time to do the work, so when I needed to know, when I needed to tap into my intuition, to understand what was happening, I received the information clearly. It wasn't magical. It's not a special psychic power. I was doing the work required to make the distinctions. One may wonder what the difference between psychic and intuitive powers is. They appear to be similar, but they are very different.

Section C

In Conclusion

Chapter 14

Intuition vs. Psychicism

Now is the time to distinguish between psychic powers and intuition. Intuition focuses on feelings. It's a natural ability with which we are all born, experience throughout our lives, and don't deny its existence. It's personal; it's within you. Unlike intuition, psychic information doesn't come from within a person but from another source, usually of spiritual origin. A psychic may experience feelings, but they're not their own feelings. Rather it's those of the spirit communicating a message. Psychic information's major difference from intuition is it comes from outside of oneself and not from one's inner higher self.

An intuitive person listens to and follows the guidance of their intuition or gut feelings. The intuitive information affects them personally because the information is specific to the person receiving it. With a psychic, the information they receive doesn't have to be about the psychic personally, but can and often be about another person. It is not personal.

Intuition is strongest in people who are mindful and practice mindfulness or meditation. They understand how to tune into their bodies to read the messages being felt. Many people experience a sense of heightened awareness or stomach pains when they know something is wrong, but they can't put their finger on it. These physical sensations are the means our intuition uses to communicate to us. Intuition is experienced all the time. For example, a suddenly inspiration to solving a problem. While a psychic must translate the insights being received from another source and give those insights meaning, intuition is immediately understood.

Psychics receive information differently. While an intuitive person physically sees, hears, and feels things with their own body a psychic goes beyond their senses, using extrasensory perception. A psychic sees without the physical eyes (clairvoyance), hears without the physical ears (clairaudience), and feels without being touched (clairsentience). The information being received is coming from a spiritual guide, so it must be deciphered in a way that makes sense to the person requesting the information from the psychic.

Most experienced psychics can turn on and off the information flow. Intuition does not shut off. It's available and continually sends useful information. As mentioned earlier, mindfulness is a powerful tool for enhancing your intuition. It also has several other benefits.

Chapter 15

Meditation

Meditation is excellent for many reasons. There are countless methods, books, and classes one can take to learn more about it. In short, mediation is a means of going into a deeper state of relaxation and awareness. Meditation allows for a clear awareness throughout the day, making interpreting Intuitive Footprints much easier. For that reason, I now address this topic.

All meditation enhances one's concentration, will power, and focus. But who has time to meditate daily? Most of us don't. My daily routine has me up at 5:00 every morning to have enough time to meditate, but I confess that sometimes, the desire to turn over and go back to sleep is just too great. Extra time is necessary if you practice concentrated mediations. In concentration, you focus on a single point, such as a mantra, prayer, or breathing, continually bringing your mind back to this single point. This requires sitting or lying quietly and steadying the mind. The places and heights your spirit can be lifted to, definitely make up for the lost sleep.

Another form of meditation, that does not require to be physically still with eyes closed, is mindfulness meditation. Mindfulness meditation is meditating while moving about in your daily life. Taking a simple exercise, like brushing your teeth, and focusing on every movement, feeling and being present in the moment. Its purpose is to keep you present in the now, second after second always completely aware of this exact moment. It is occurring without interpretation. Mindful meditation is the most powerful way to add meditating to your life without losing sleep because you don't have to find the time. Mindfulness is being mindful of something occurring in the present moment.

Don't be fooled into thinking mindfulness is easier than concentration meditation. They both are powerful and require a great deal of commitment to gain any meaningful benefits. There's too much to learn and speak about meditation. It goes way beyond the scope of this book. It would be best to read about the different methods and start somewhere with a simple meditation practice. It will help in your daily life, and it will enhance your intuition.

Chapter 16

A Final Word

Our intuition is a natural state; it's always providing information. It's up to us to retrieve the information and put it to use. Paying attention and using it will make it flow quicker and stronger. Imagine your intuition is really your grandmother. You visit her and ask her advice about how to stay married as long as she and your grandfather have. She stops everything she's doing to provide her wisdom. Your grandmother shares her insights and love before she sends you on your way. After a few weeks, your grandmother notices that you're not doing anything she suggested; in fact, it's as if she never spoke to you in the first place.

Several months later, you come to your grandmother again and in your very excited way you ask her to share her wisdom on how to stay happily married for all those years. This time, your grandmother doesn't stop what she's doing right away, but after completing her task, she sits and shares everything with you. This time, it takes your grandmother a little longer to get excited because she already shared all this information with you before, and you simply ignored it. Again, you leave and proceed not to take any of her advice, as if she never shared any of her wisdom with you.

Well, on your third trip to visit grandmother to request her wisdom, do you really think she's going to pay much attention to your request? She may throw a small tidbit or two at you while she continues to do what she was doing before your arrival. She's not going to waste her time, until she sees you're serious and start applying the valuable information she's putting in front of you.

Well, our intuition is just like grandmother. It will come on demand and not stop at anything to help you get the message clearly, unless you don't honor the information you receive. If after asking for intuitive insight, you simply ignore the advice, it will eventually not appear on demand. It will have to be coaxed often and shown by your use of its messages that you're serious. Then it comes easily again.

No major decision should be based totally on intuition, but the information provided intuitively must not be ignored either. It's best to have all the information possibly available to you, including intuition, before making any important decision. Enhancing our intuition and learning to connect to our inner-net of intuition can lead us to a spiritual path, even if that's not our original intention. The continuous Relax and Stepping Back begins to transform the chatter in our minds to a more quiet, still place, where Silence can be heard. The Lord speaks to us in that "Still, small voice" (1 Kings 19:12) which is heard more easily because you silence the chatter. As Eckhart Tolle wrote in *Stillness Speaks,* "When you lose touch with inner stillness, you lose touch with yourself. When you lose touch with yourself, you lose yourself in the world. Your innermost sense of self, of who you are, is inseparable from stillness."

The success of retrieving or accessing the inner-net of intuition is largely affected by one's intention. Intentions are created in this mental field. Throughout these many exercises, have the intent to succeed. Have the intent to have fun and experiment. Have the imagination and freedom of a child. All these exercises are done from within. There's nothing holding you back, except the wrong intention. So take a moment, review your intention, and declare out loud to yourself, "I will succeed in tapping into my inner-net of intuition on demand. I will enjoy experimenting with these exercises and learning the techniques that will propel me forward in several areas of my life."

Now, go do so.

References

Braud, W. (2000). Wellness implications of retroactive intentional influence: Exploring an outrageous hypothesis. *Alternative Therapies in Health and Medicine* *6*(1), 37-48. Retrieved from http://www.inclusivepsychology.com/uploads/WellnessImplicationsOf RetroactiveIntentionalInfluence.pdf

Shafica Karagulla, M.D. (1967). *Breakthrough to Creativity you Higher Sense Perception* Marina del Rey, CA: Book Graphics, Inc.

Targ, R. (2010). *Limitless Mind.* San Francisco, CA: New World Library. Edgar Cayce and John Van Auken (2007). *Toward a Deeper Meditation.* Virginia Beach, VA: A.R.E. Press

Carol Ann Liaros (2003). *Intuition Made Easy.* Scottsdale, AZ: Cloudbank Creations, Inc.

Malachi Martin (1976). *Hostage to the Devil.* New York, NY: Harper Collins

Eckhart Tolle (2003) *Stillness Speaks.* Vancouver, Canada: Namaste Publishing

Kevin J. Todeschi (2003). *Dreams Images and Symbols A Dictionary.* Virginia Beach, VA: A.R.E. Press

Appendix A

The Lord's Prayer

Our Father in heaven, hallowed be your name. Your kingdom come, your will be done, on earth as it is in heaven. Give us this day our daily bread, and forgive us our debts, as we also have forgiven our debtors. And lead us not into temptation, but deliver us from evil. Matthew 6:9–13 (ESV)

Appendix B

Saint Michael the Archangel Prayer

St. Michael the Archangel, defend us in battle.

Be our defense against the wickedness and snares of the Devil.

May God rebuke him, we humbly pray, and do thou, O Prince of the heavenly hosts, by the power of God, thrust into hell Satan, and all the evil spirits, who prowl about the world seeking the ruin of souls. Amen.

Appendix C

Chakras

Chakra's Name	Etheric Body Organs and glands fed by corresponding chakra	Astral Body Emotion
Root	Reproductive organs	A person's understanding of the foundation of existence. Does one feel safe or not in this world
Spleen	Spleen gland	Fear, sadness, insecurity
Solar plexus	adrenal glands, liver, pancreas, gallbladder, kidneys, stomach, digestive system, sympathetic nervous system	Personal power One's understanding of family

Heart	heart and thymus gland	love, compassion, understanding and peacefulness
Throat	thyroid gland	decision making free will creativity and self-expression
Crown	Pineal gland and brain	Intuitive and spiritual development
Third eye	Pituitary gland and hypothalamus	precognitive center

Appendix D
Outline of Body Images

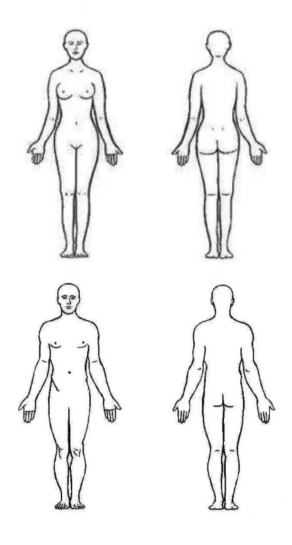

Appendix E
Author's Personal
Intuitive Footprints™

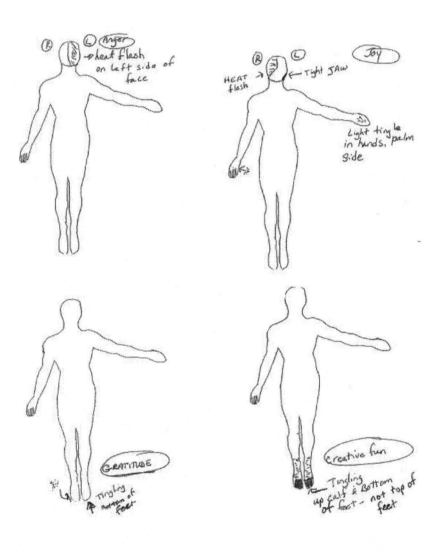

Appendix F

Aura Colors

Color	Positive Traits When Bright, Brilliant or Vibrant	Negative Traits When Dull, Murky, or Dim
Black	Emotional deep, beautiful, glamour, efficient	Oppressive, cold, malicious, negativity, sin
Blue	Intuitive and have strong spiritual power to draw upon. High degree of spirituality. Intelligence, good communication, trust, logic	Aloofness, unfriendly, bitter holding resentment, sadness
Brown	Warmth, nurturing, abundance, practical	Heaviness, cold, lacking
Gray	Neutral, calming, mysterious	Illness, lack of energy, depression, boredom
Green	Balance, restorative, peaceful, harmonious, healing	Stagnate, angry, jealous, envious, green with envy
Orange	Organized, security, creativity, abundance, physical comfort	Chaos, scarcity, frivolity, immaturity
Pink	Nurturing, warmth, sexual, feminine	Inhibition, Jezebel spirit, emasculation
Red	energy, power, passion, love, excitement, masculine, warmth	force, desire, danger, strain, cruel

Silver	Wisdom, maturity, resources, eloquent	Frail, weak emotionally and mentally, misleading
White	Clarity, purity, perfection	Coldness, unfriendly, sterile
Violet/ Purple	Spiritual awareness, royalty, caregiver, assist in community needs beyond self, mastery.	Sense of entitlement, selfishness
Yellow	Optimist, confident, extrovert, giving, generous, warm, intelligence, power, developing spiritual qualities	Pessimist, introvert, selfish, cold, withholding

Appendix G
Energy Ball Table

Date/Time	Frequency	Strength	Temp.	Pressure	Location	Mood
7AM						
8AM						
9AM						
10 AM						
11 AM						
Noon						
1 PM						
2 PM						
3 PM						
4 PM						
5 PM						
6 PM						
7 PM						
8 PM						
9 PM						
10 PM						
11 PM						

About the Author

After many years of assisting with healings and clearings, Nora Truscello realized that many people didn't understand the inherent dangers of being a healer, psychic, or spiritual worker. She began a mission to educate others in the field about how to protect themselves from evil. This book is part of that journey which was begun last year when she published her first book, *The Spiritual Psychic: 4 Necessary Steps for Healers and Lightworkers to Protect Against Evil and Demons.* She ranked #1 Best Seller in Mysticism on Amazon and recently #1 in Good vs. Evil Philosophy.

Nora has over 25 years of experience and training in the psychic, spiritual realm. Her expertise has been proven time and time again through her delivery of exceptionally accurate psychic readings. She has been conducting lectures on a wide variety of subjects for the last decade. Nora's core competencies include; Psychometry, Remote viewing, Cleansing and Clearing negative energies, Sensing Auras, Spirit Communication, and using Energy Medicine along with psychic abilities.

Nora lives in Philadelphia with her husband Anthony. She is the mother of three grown sons and the proud grandmother of two precious grandsons.

Questions about this material, other topics or author can be addressed to: Nora@SecretsOfIntuition.com or on our website at SecretsOfIntuition.com